MORE
IDITAROD CLASSICS

Tales of the Trail Told by the
Men & Women Who Race Across Alaska

MORE IDITAROD CLASSICS

Tales of the Trail Told by the
Men & Women Who Race Across Alaska

Lew Freedman
Author of the best-selling IDITAROD CLASSICS

Illustrations by Jon Van Zyle

EPICENTER PRESS
Alaska Book Adventures™

Epicenter Press is a regional press founded in Alaska whose interests include but are not limited to the arts, history, environment, and diverse cultures and lifestyles of the Pacific Northwest and high latitudes. We seek both the traditional and innovative in publishing nonfiction books, and contemporary art and photography gift books.

Publisher: Kent Sturgis
Acquisitions Editor: Lael Morgan
Cover and book design: Newman Design/Illustration
Editor: Susan Ohrberg
Printer: Transcontinental Printing
Text ©2004 Lew Freedman
Illustrations ©2004 Jon Van Zyle

Library of Congress Control Number 2004102295
ISBN 0-9724944-8-0

Booksellers: This title is available from major wholesalers. Retail discounts are available from our trade distributor, Graphic Arts Center Publishing Co., PO Box 10306, Portland, OR 97210.

First Printing, March 2004
10 9 8 7 6 5 4 3 2

PRINTED IN CANADA

To order a single copy of MORE IDITAROD CLASSICS, mail $14.95 plus $6.00 for shipping and handling (WA residents add $1.90 state sales tax) to: Epicenter Press, PO Box 82368, Kenmore, WA 98028.

Discover exciting ALASKA BOOK ADVENTURES! Visit our online Alaska bookstore at www.EpicenterPress.com, or call our 24-hour, toll-free hotline at 800-950-6663. Visit our online gallery featuring official Iditarod artist Jon Van Zyle at www.JonVanZyle.com.

DEDICATION

This book is dedicated to Iditarod musher Bob Ernisse, who brought so much joy to so many people.

Other Epicenter Press titles from Lew Freedman

Diamonds in the Rough
Father of the Iditarod
Fishing for a Laugh
Iditarod Classics
Iditarod Dreams
Iditarod Silver
One Second to Glory
Spirit of the Wind

TABLE OF CONTENTS

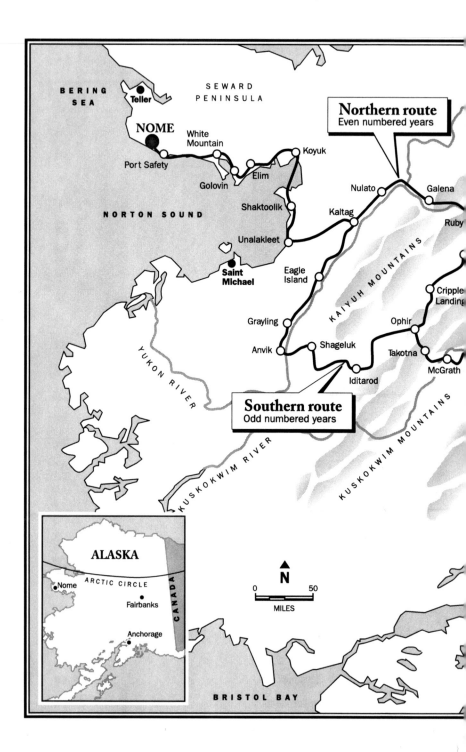

IDITAROD TRAIL SLED DOG RACE

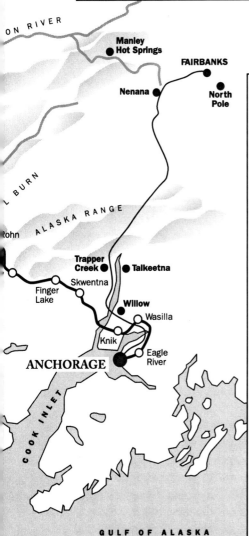

UKUK RIVER

ON RIVER

Manley Hot Springs

FAIRBANKS

Nenana

North Pole

L BURN

ALASKA RANGE

Rohn

Trapper Creek

Talkeetna

Skwentna

Finger Lake

Willow

Wasilla

Knik

Eagle River

ANCHORAGE

COOK INLET

GULF OF ALASKA

Iditarod checkpoint mileage

O Checkpoints:	Mileage
Anchorage to Eagle River	20
Eagle River to Wasilla	29
Wasilla to Knik	14
Knik to Skwentna	88
Skwentna to Finger Lake	45
Finger Lake to Rainy Pass	30
Rainy Pass to Rohn	40
Rohn to Nikolai	93
Nikolai to McGrath	48
McGrath to Takotna	23
Takotna to Ophir	38
SOUTHERN ROUTE	
Ophir to Iditarod	90
Iditarod to Shageluk	65
Shageluk to Anvik	25
Anvik to Grayling	18
Grayling to Eagle Island	70
Eagle Island to Kaltag	70
Kaltag to Unalakleet	90
Unalakleet to Shaktoolik	38
Shaktoolik to Koyuk	58
Koyuk to Elim	48
Elim to Golovin	28
Golovin to White Mountain	18
White Mountain to Port Safety	55
Port Safety to **Nome**	22
NORTHERN ROUTE	
Ophir to Cripple	60
Cripple to Sulatna	45
Sulatna to Ruby	75
Ruby to Galena	52
Galena to Nulato	52
Nulato to Kaltag	42

INTRODUCTION

Iditarod Classics: Tales of the Trail Told by the Men and Women Who Race Across Alaska first appeared in print in 1992. In the twelve years since, the Iditarod Trail Sled Dog Race has grown in popularity, establishing itself in the minds of not only Alaskans but also other Americans and Europeans as perhaps the world's greatest adventure endurance race.

On the first Saturday in March, men and women gather on Fourth Avenue in downtown Anchorage before a roaring crowd, and set out to cross 1,100 miles of some of the coldest, roughest terrain on earth. The journey for these mushers, accompanied only by the huskies they've raised and trained, is unique each time. No one knows what the winter and weather will bring, what challenges the trip down the trail will provide. The race is always a journey of self-discovery, a challenge to the body and spirit and the limits of teamwork.

Those who complete "The Last Great Race" are admired as Alaska's major sporting heroes. The Iditarod is a throwback, an event that harkens back to an earlier, more basic time, and it is well known that it takes special skills merely to get where you want to go in Alaska.

More Iditarod Classics is about twenty-four men and women who have tackled the trail; about mushers who dare to be great; about mushers whose exploits have captivated the public.

Included are the three multiple champions of the last dozen years: Martin Buser, Jeff King, and Doug Swingley—the Montanan who not only became the first musher from outside Alaska to win the Iditarod but also won it three more times.

Included are mushers whose poignant tales reveal the obstacles they battled merely to reach the starting line, and how they persevered to cross the finish line.

Included are mushers who explain why they keep coming back to this unique event year after year, even if they aren't likely to join the elite roster of champions.

Having spent more than twenty years observing and absorbing the Iditarod, and fifteen years interviewing its winners, contenders, and back-of-the-packers, I have grown attached to the drama of the race and the hardiness of the people and dogs who make it great. These are stories of hardship and glory, but above all, of a steadfast belief in a distinctive, extraordinary sporting event that each year for about two weeks inspires all who come into contact with it.

Welcome to the Iditarod Trail.

— Lew Freedman

RACE RECORD

| 1973 | 31 days, 11 hours, 59 minutes | 20th |

CHAPTER 1
HOWARD FARLEY

It took Howard Farley, seventy-one, of Nome, more than a month to complete the first Iditarod Trail Sled Dog Race in 1973 when he was already an old-timer of forty, but it was one of the grandest months of his life.

Farley spent months helping Iditarod founding father Joe Redington Sr. plan and organize the race, working to make it a reality. He cherishes a letter Redington sent to him in December 1972 that in part added Farley to the Iditarod Trail Committee.

Probably the first musher to give tourists dogsled rides in Alaska, Farley was raised in the Seattle area and came to the old gold rush town of Nome to be a butcher. He got his start in the sport when the grocery store he worked for decided it would be a great gimmick to deliver orders by dog team.

During the 1970s, Farley gave ten thousand rides a year to visitors; he maintained his tour business until 2000. Farley raced the Iditarod only once, but he gathered enough material to regale tourists for three decades.

T he first Iditarod, that's something they'll never be able to take away from me. We were basically a cross-section of Alaska's rural guys, with only a few city guys. Joe Redington announced that we were going to award a $50,000 purse. In 1973 that was a lot of money. It was unheard of. Everybody had been racing for trophies and a few hundred dollars.

You wouldn't believe the people who said it couldn't be done. They said, "This thing will never go. You don't have the money." I looked at the whole thing a little differently. I thought, This is the greatest thing that ever came along for Alaska. I believed in it. I thought it didn't have a chance of failing. All my life I've told the tourists, "I looked at it as P. T. Barnum. It was the greatest show for Alaska. That's what it was."

The first time I met Joe Redington, he was working at the fish processing plant in Unalakleet. It was the summer of 1972. I had heard of him and he had heard of me. I knew him because he organized the first race called the Iditarod, in 1967, for the Alaska Centennial. When Joe met me, he said, "I know who you are. You're that crazy guy up there in Nome who runs a big dog team for the tourists."

He started telling me about this dog race to Nome that he was planning, and I got involved. We talked on the telephone for months. For years the only time anyone could get in touch with Joe Redington was after midnight. I had a lot of $700 phone bills. There was no one to reimburse me. Joe was Don Quixote, striking at windmills.

I went into Anchorage two weeks ahead of the race. I stayed at Joe's, and we drove into town every day. That's about sixty miles. We promoted all day long, trying to raise money. Joe didn't eat and he didn't sleep. We would start out at 8 AM and head home at 2 or 3 AM.

I don't think anybody really trained for the first Iditarod. No one had ever done a race of that distance. We figured if we traveled slowly enough, we could train the dogs as we went. That's why it took us so darned long to finish. Dick Wilmarth was the winner, and it took him twenty days.

Before we set out, there wasn't much fanfare. It was a tough sell. A lot of people figured this would not work. Even the guys in the sprint-mushing community didn't believe in us. They were saying, "You're going to go out there and die." The only people who were there for the start at Tudor Track in Anchorage were a few of the wives and sweethearts.

I started with fifteen dogs, and I was driving a 13½-foot sled. A huge freight sled. People asked me how I was going to get it through the trees. It cost me $175. A few years later the same thing cost $600. It must have weighed a hundred pounds. It was really funny what we thought we would need. Nobody knew, so we packed too heavily. I left stuff all along the way.

I wasn't a racer. I had never been in a dog race in my life. I had driven dogs for miles and miles, and I never had a fear of driving a big team, but we had no idea what this thing would be. The funny thing is, when he signed up, Dick Wilmarth visited Joe and said, "I think I've got this thing figured out." He was a miner, and he was hoping to win enough money for a backhoe. He won and never raced the Iditarod again.

I was the thirty-first racer off the starting line, with Wilmarth just ahead of me. I got all screwed up, though, all turned around, and I never saw him again. We mushed along the side of the road from Anchorage through Eagle River. It was warm out, in the thirties, with not much snow there. I was dressed in furs and my dogs all had heavy fur. I was waving at people, and the steel runners were throwing up sparks.

Even though there wasn't much excitement in Alaska, I had a contract with the *Seattle Times* to write stories and take pictures. I thought, Boy, I'm in fat city. It wasn't as grandiose as I thought it would be, though. Only about half of the pictures came out.

I was in fifteenth place when I got into the checkpoint at Knik, and I got a good rest. These days the mushers don't even stop in Knik. I spent the night, and when I woke up in the morning, they were all gone. Vi Redington, Joe's wife, was there, and she said, "Let me cook you some breakfast." That was the first time, but not the last, that I wondered just how much of a race it was.

As I got into Yentna, it was pretty foggy. I hooked up with Dr. Hal Bartko. Joe had given us a rinky-dink map and the distances weren't that accurate, but I knew I was getting close to Skwentna. I carried a .45 pistol because we didn't know if the bears would come out looking for a meal. Trying to see the right way to go, I climbed up on the sled. But I dropped the pistol in the snow and lost it.

Doc Bartko had forgotten his thick boots, and the word got passed back to Joe. The going was tough, and then we heard a noise near Finger Lake. It was Joe in his plane. He dropped that plane right down in a meadow, climbed out, and said, "Here's Doc's bunny boots."

The whole race was start and stop. We just had to take it one day at a time. It didn't get really cold until we got to McGrath. There it was sixty below. They had hot food for us at checkpoints, but when I went into the bunkhouse and lifted the lid on the pot, it didn't look very appetizing. I said, "God, I guess this is what we've got to eat."

Tex Gates, an old-timer, lived there, and his wife invited me to the house. I had some moose stew and pancakes. But it was so hot in there. It felt like 110 degrees. Tex talked all night, and I got about one hour's sleep. Finally, I said, "I've got to get out of here."

By the time I got to Ruby, I was in last place. A guy said, "This is a dry town, but how would you like to have a drink?" Then he handed me a pint of Seagram's 7. They told me people were wondering where I was because I had been out of touch. I had been out of touch for 5½ days, they said, but I didn't think I had been out of touch. I saw all kinds of pilots fly overhead and wiggle their wings. They saw me.

I had caught up to a few other mushers at the checkpoint, and we were in Ruby when we heard the finish on the radio, that Wilmarth had come in. Some of the guys said they thought they should quit. But by the time I got to Ruby, I figured we might as well go on. I said, "I don't know about you guys, but I'm going home."

The sun was out. Things were looking up. A lot of mushers scratched, but I didn't intend to be one of them. We set the tone for the future of the Iditarod, where the mushers in the back of the pack are as important as the frontrunners. Unbeknownst to us at the time, you were a hero even if you just finished the race.

It took me thirty-one days, but nowadays I think I could do it in fifteen, knowing what people know about long-distance mushing.

When I came around Cape Nome, on the outskirts of town, a good friend of mine came out on his snowmachine and flagged me down. He said, "Boy, are we glad to see you." He gave me a little, bitty red lantern—the symbol of the last-place finisher—and he said, "Are you gonna be last?" I said, "I hope not."

Bruce Mitchell was still out there, and I knew John Schultz was behind me. My dogs picked up speed. When I pulled in on Front Street, people were cheering, but the gal who was the checker, Pam Randles, leaned over to me and whispered in my ear, "You're not officially over the line." We had to move the whole crowd over about ten feet. I was twentieth, and I won $500. Schultz was last.

I got a big reception. Spectators carried me around on their shoulders because I was the hometown guy. Most of us just wanted to finish. The Iditarod is so much faster now, with the winner finishing in fewer than ten days. But I think the race has gone the right way. It should be everyone's race, and it still is. We get women. We get men. We get people from all over the world in it.

I haven't raced in the Iditarod in more than thirty years, and I gave up my dogs a couple of years ago, but I have never missed watching the winner come in and I have never missed one of the finishers' banquets in Nome.

The Iditarod's world famous these days, but I'm not surprised. I knew it would be that big. It had the makings of a great event. Back in the beginning, it was just a dream. It outgrew all of us, and look at it now.

RACE RECORD

1975	14 days, 14 hours, 43 minutes	1st
1976	19 days, 5 hours, 10 minutes	5th
1977	16 days, 19 hours, 57 minutes	4th
1978	14 days, 19 hours, 28 minutes	3rd
1979	15 days, 11 hours, 19 minutes	2nd
1980	15 days, 16 hours, 14 minutes	9th
1981	13 days, 14 hours, 14 minutes	12th
1982	16 days, 5 hours, 6 minutes	4th
1983	14 days, 3 hours, 36 minutes	19th
1984	14 days, 15 hours, 8 minutes	17th
1985	18 days, 23 hours, 21 minutes	12th
1990	15 days, 21 hours, 11 minutes	41st
1992	Scratched	
2000	12 days, 2 hours, 42 minutes	40th

CHAPTER 2
EMMITT PETERS

Emmitt Peters, sixty-four, grew up in a family of dog mushers in the Yukon River village of Ruby. The man later nicknamed "The Yukon Fox" got his first dog, Red, when he was seven.

Peters' first family responsibility involved driving a dogsled to the wood yard three miles away to bring back firewood. By age thirteen, Peters used a dog team to mush to school. In summer, huge quantities of chum salmon were caught and dried, then stored for winter dog food in the predominantly Native community.

For about eight years in the 1960s, Peters lived in Los Angeles, Portland, and Seattle. But when he tired of city life, he returned home and began racing dogs. In the early 1970s, Peters trained his father Paul's dogs and entered the Fur Rendezvous World Championship Sled Dog Race in Anchorage.

After a few mediocre performances, he received advice from world champion Dr. Roland Lombard that changed his life. Lombard told Peters his big, tough dogs were better suited to the long-distance Iditarod.

Unheralded, Peters entered the same team of dogs in the 1975 Iditarod and captured the title, becoming the first and only musher to win the Iditarod as a rookie. His speedy victory is credited with transforming the Iditarod from a camping trip to a true race.

Talking to Doc, that really inspired me. That was how I got the idea I could do the Iditarod. The longest I had trained my dogs was fifty miles. I thought to myself, By golly, if I go fifty or sixty miles a day, I'll be right near the top. I only had twelve of my own dogs, so I borrowed two more from musher Vern Cherneski, and two more from local people in Ruby.

At the start, I was nervous. I didn't want to take the lead. I was busy worrying about how I was going to keep up with the top-notch mushers. But at first I was holding the brake a lot, trying to stay behind them. The dogs were getting a lot of rest. I was staying eight or ten hours at a lot of those early checkpoints.

I was catching guys four or five times. It became obvious that my dogs were faster than most of theirs. I had always said that if you could do the Iditarod with sprint dogs and keep them happy, it would be a faster race. I wasn't four hours on the trail, and I stopped. That was my race plan. And that was when everyone caught me. But then I would get ahead again. That was the start of using speed dogs. Before that, they had camping dogs.

The terrain was all different for me. I thought there was no end to this race. It was brand new to me, going a thousand miles. When you get out there on long stretches without villages, there's nothing but mountains and ice.

When we got to McGrath, about four hundred miles into the race, I was sixth, behind Herbert (Nayokpuk), Joe (Redington) Sr., Jerry Riley, Henry Beatus, and Carl Huntington. By the time we got to Ruby, I was third. The others had taken their twenty-four-hour layover in Rohn, Nikolai, or McGrath. I waited. I was the last one. I decided to take it in Ruby because it was home. I didn't think it would turn out that way, that I could do it.

I only had eight dogs left after leaving McGrath. I wanted to rest them good, and Ruby seemed like the best place. When I got there, Joe Sr. and Joee Redington Jr. had come in and gone. It was thirty-five degrees below zero, and I was lucky I didn't run into a snowstorm; it was behind me.

In the early days of the Iditarod, before they passed the corral-ling rule, people could help you in the checkpoints and you could

sleep in private homes. My dad
and my brothers cooked the dog
food and took care of the dogs.
That was one good advantage. I
was trying to sleep, but my mother,
Mary, didn't understand that I was
on my layover. She kept waking
me up every two hours, saying
about the other mushers, "They're
leaving. They're leaving."

I left Ruby at about 11:30 at
night. About eight miles down the Yukon River is my fish camp. I
was worried that the dogs were going to turn off there and wouldn't
leave. But they went past the turnoff. After about fifty-two miles,
I stopped and made myself a little nest. I sat down inside the sled,
put on my parka, and went to sleep.

I woke up about six o'clock in the morning, and I was only about
ten miles from Galena. I was well rested. There were about twenty
mushers ahead of me because of my twenty-four-hour layover, but
I caught a lot of them in Galena. I started picking them off. My
lead dog, Nugget, had won for Carl Huntington in 1974. She knew
where to go on the trail.

When I got into Nulato in the evening, there were about eight
mushers still ahead of me. I was really making time. I passed a
couple more headed into Kaltag. I was up to fifth place. The dogs
were doing well. We were clipping along, going about twelve miles
an hour.

The leaders were just checking out of Unalakleet when I was
pulling in. All the time, I knew I was gaining on them. I mushed
on to Koyuk, and there was Joe Sr. camped on the ice, sleeping in
his sleeping bag. He woke up and said, "Who goes there?" When
I told him, he said, "Wait for me." I went around him, but I waited
for him. When we started mushing, though, I pulled away.

I got into Koyuk about six o'clock in the morning, but I didn't
want the other mushers to know. I checked in, then I started my
Coleman stove. I melted snow and warmed up some beaver meat.
Nobody knew I was there. I walked into the checkpoint, and Joee Jr.
was sound asleep in his sleeping bag. Jerry Riley was climbing into
his sleeping bag for a rest. He kicked Herbert and said, "Emmitt's

here." They packed up right away and moved on. But I stayed and rested for four hours.

By the time they got all of their gear packed and started out, they had a 2½-hour lead on me. But I caught up to them again going into Elim. It was obvious that my dogs were moving faster. Herbert came over to me and said, "It looks like it's between you and Jerry." He was going to hang back and take a long rest. So I moved up to second place.

Jerry went on. Going up to Golovin, I caught up to Jerry again. We were neck and neck the twenty miles all the way from Golovin to White Mountain. White Mountain is seventy-seven miles from Nome. I was trying to come up with an edge. I tried to figure out how I could carry some extra food for my dogs on the sled. I knew there would be no more time to cook.

I asked the checker if he could find a five-gallon bucket so I could carry beaver meat and broth. I wrapped my sleeping bag around the bucket to keep it from freezing. We had a clear sky, but along the Bering Sea coast it was ten below zero.

Jerry was about 2½ hours ahead of me out of White Mountain, but I caught him about three miles outside of Solomon, thirty miles from Nome. I knew he was going to be the man to beat because when I passed the others, I just ran away from them. Jerry kept hanging in there. This time he waved at me to go on by.

When I reached Solomon, there were Orville Lake and Dick Tozier, who were more famous as officials at the Fur Rondy, doing radio commentary. They were on the air, and when they saw a dog team approach, they said, "Ladies and gentlemen, here's the first musher, Jerry Riley."

I mushed up to them and said, "No, I'm Emmitt Peters. Jerry's back there." They said, "Ladies and gentlemen, we've got a new leader, the Yukon Fox." They gave me the nickname right then and there. That's how I got the nickname, and it's stuck to me ever since.

I stopped to feed the dogs the beaver and the broth, and Jerry mushed up to me. He was surprised. "You carried that all this way?" he said. He had frozen beaver meat and his dogs were having trouble chewing it.

After that, I pushed hard all the way into Nome. I ran and pushed for thirty miles. I was sure I was the fastest, but I knew Jerry wouldn't give up. That was as hard as I'd worked in my whole life.

With only eight dogs left, I did a lot of running. I was sweating.

Wow. Coming into Nome, I could see people on both sides of the street all the way out to the Fort Davis Roadhouse. That's a couple of miles from the finish line. People were yelling and screaming. There were thousands of people. That was just so exciting. I got so darned excited I forgot how tired I was. The dogs were really clipping, and I was running hard.

After I came down Front Street, the people lifted me up and carried me all around. I said I needed to buy my dogs T-bone steaks as a reward, and the Alaska Commercial store gave each of the dogs a steak.

When I finally went home with the people I was staying with, I took a hot shower and fell asleep. At three o'clock in the morning, they heard me moving around. I was putting on my boots. I said, "I've got to get back on the trail and catch up to those guys." They said, "Emmitt, the race is over." And I fell right back into bed.

It was a thrill to win the Iditarod. It meant that I had finally completed my dream. I dreamed I was going to get into the big race, and I accomplished it. I had only come in tenth in the Fur Rendezvous, and I had never done anything great like this. It meant a lot to me. It opened up a whole world to me.

The next year, Jerry Riley won. He got back at me. I was fifth. It took him four days longer, too. I was really proud of my winning time. And so far, I'm the last rookie to win the race. It will be hard to beat that.

Now when the mushers come through Ruby, I watch them and visualize where I've been. I follow the race on television, and when they come into Ruby I'm always involved. I'm a lot older, but I help the Iditarod. In 1975 I was full of energy. It seems like it was yesterday.

It's a great feeling when people still call me "Iditarod champion." I just had the dogs. It was the right time. And I had Nugget. She was a great dog. In 1977 I was training my dogs in Anchorage, and she slipped her harness and got away from me. She ran off and got hit by a car and was killed. Nugget was going on ten years old. I had her cremated and I've still got her ashes.

RACE RECORD

| 1976 | 26 days, 8 hours, 42 minutes | 33rd |
| 1979 | 22 days, 13 hours, 50 minutes | 42nd |

CHAPTER 3

JON VAN ZYLE

An internationally acclaimed artist, Jon Van Zyle, sixty-one, of Eagle River, Alaska, has been associated with the Iditarod for more than three decades. Race fans eagerly await the late-winter release of his annual Iditarod poster and print. A long-time dog musher and a sometime racer, Van Zyle, and his twin brother, Daniel, also a painter, were born in Northern Michigan, lived in upstate New York, and settled in Colorado with their mother, Ruth, in the late 1950s.

Throughout high school, Van Zyle and his brother talked of moving to Alaska. Instead, he was introduced to hunting, fishing, and Siberian huskies in Lakewood, Colorado, before finally making the move to Alaska in 1971. Van Zyle's mother raised, trained, and bred collies, so he was always around working dogs. The influence of the *Alaska Sportsman* magazine contributed to his desire to own huskies.

It was Van Zyle's long association with Sears, Roebuck in Hawaii and the Pacific Northwest that earned him a transfer to Anchorage. For years, Van Zyle worked for Sears by day and painted landscapes, wildlife, and other outdoor scenes at night. Van Zyle acquired a few Siberian huskies while living in Portland, Oregon, and his current kennel remains true to the breed.

In the winter of 1972, a good friend of mine, Darrell Reynolds, and I were training dogs together at the Tudor Track in Anchorage, and Joe Redington Sr. came by. At that time, dog mushers knew who Joe Redington was but no one else did.

In those days I was entering sprint races and traveling with my dogs in the backcountry. We got to talking, and Joe mentioned that he was going to hold this Iditarod race. I think we passed out photocopied notices for him.

Darrell and I were just doing our thing. We would take weekend-long trips out of Cantwell, visiting friends. I was working for Sears as display sales manager. When Joe talked about a long-distance race, it struck a real bell. I didn't really like sprints. It didn't make sense to me to train and train and train and have the race be over in ten minutes or forty minutes.

I know some people said a thousand-mile race couldn't be done, but it never entered my mind that it was too far. I preferred mushing in the backcountry. I get excited in my own way when a challenge is presented. To me it was no big deal.

The first year of the race, 1973, they had some kind of rule where you could have two drivers, either as a team or a backup of some kind. Brothers Robert and Owen Ivan raced as a team. Well, Darrell signed up and I signed up with him, just in case something happened to him.

On the day the race started, there we were at Tudor Track, with about twelve other people and a few mushers. As Darrell mushed toward Eagle River, I met him at the railroad crossing in Eklutna and at the Knik River Bridge with my car. There was traffic, and the dog teams needed help crossing the bridge. I remember to this day that when I saw Dick Wilmarth—nobody knew him at the time—and his dog team, I said, "That guy is going to win, or die trying." The dogs were just flat moving. They were going so fast that in order to try and control them, he turned the sled over sideways and rode sidesaddle. And Wilmarth did win the race.

There wasn't any snow. It was all dirt. And I helped Darrell cross the bridge. It was good to have a handler there. That was the last I saw of him. I went about my business for the rest of the day and

didn't get home until late. The next morning, I heard from Darrell. He called to say
he had pneumonia and had scratched and
where was I. He had been looking for me
to take over the team and mush to Nome.
To this day I kick myself, because I would
have taken over that dog team in the first
Iditarod and I wasn't home.

I knew I would mush the Iditarod from
the first time Joe Redington talked to us. I
just could not get my dog team together in good enough fashion for
the first one. In 1974 I couldn't put enough training miles on them.
I probably didn't have enough good dogs, either. In 1975 I talked to
my boss early on and told him I was taking my vacation to do the
Iditarod. I had the miles in training and everything was a go. At
the last minute, when I reminded my boss that I was going to be off
for a month, I was told, no, I couldn't go. There was an important
company visitor coming from headquarters. I was not happy.

I quit a little bit later. My departure from Sears was connected
to the fact that I wanted to do the Iditarod in 1976. I had also been
painting for a number of years, and my income from the painting
had matched my income from Sears for about a year.

I had been painting and drawing my whole life. Sometime in
the mid-1960s, I went to a paint store and they had tubes of acrylic
paints. I bought a tube of black and a tube of white. That's kind of
what got me going with acrylics.

Although my art specialty has been outdoor scenes, the lure of
Alaska had nothing to do with art. I've always gravitated to outdoor
things. I enjoyed taking off for two hundred miles by dog team just
to see someone. The Iditarod was so intriguing because I wanted to
prove that my dogs could do that. I knew what kind of dogs it took
mentally to do that kind of thing. Darrell entered again in 1975,
and I put all of my efforts into helping him finish twentieth.

I got my chance to enter the Iditarod in 1976. I may not always
sound like a positive person when I'm talking, but I never go into
anything assuming I'm not going to get there. I'm a driven, determined person when I set my mind to it. I never had any doubts
my dogs would get there. But to me it was about the pure joy of
doing it.

It didn't occur to me that I couldn't win. It didn't occur to me that I could be last. Or be in the middle. Finishing was the most important thing. Really, the only thing that I'm competitive in is my art. If I was nervous, it was probably at the starting line. I don't really get nervous. I may get hectic. Stan Smith, who later did the Iditarod, asked me, "Do you ever get nervous?" No, but I may say, "Get out of my way, I need to get this done."

A thousand-mile race was new to me. The dogs can fail you and you can fail the dogs. But the Iditarod lived up to my expectations. After the first three nights had gone by, it was gorgeous, cold and clear, and I remember thinking, "This is what it's all about."

I started the race with fourteen dogs. That was the most we could start with at the time. I dropped four of them before I got to Finger Lake, but that's all I dropped. I was worried, but I figured out how to run the dogs better. We had time. In the 1970s it took a week to get to McGrath, four hundred miles into the race.

It was during this race that I hooked up with Dennis Corrington, who became one of my best friends. We were kind of the middle end of the pack and ran into some hellacious storms. In those days they only put the trail in once, for the frontrunners. I trained my dogs to get them tough. I think maybe I trained them too slowly. But it worked out because the conditions were so tough.

Dennis was from Nome and he knew Darrell, so I knew Dennis vicariously before the race. We would see each other occasionally at a checkpoint, and Dennis left Rainy Pass shortly after I did. About seven or eight miles out, there was a tent set up for sheep hunters. I snacked my dogs there. I was just about to leave when Dennis pulled in, and we started talking. We looked at the weather and saw that a bad storm was coming in through Ptarmigan Pass, so we decided to stick together. We basically stayed together the whole time after that.

We passed mushers, but they all dropped out after we passed them. Somewhere on the Bering Sea coast we found out we were running last. It didn't matter. Dennis and I were doing the Iditarod to satisfy ourselves. I finished the race in 26 days, 8 hours, 42 minutes, 42 seconds. Dennis was nine seconds behind me and won the Red Lantern. We did beat the thirteen people who dropped out.

Doing the Iditarod was great. I came home, and because it was such a moving experience, I wanted to paint it. I did twenty paintings about the race and had a show at The Gallery in Anchorage. The show was very successful, and somewhere along the way I got the wild hare to do something that would let other people know about the race.

I contacted the Iditarod and talked to Gail Phillips, who was the treasurer of the Iditarod Trail Committee. We discussed doing a poster. Just one. I talked to Dorothy Page, who was known as the Mother of the Iditarod, and she said to do it.

I didn't have much money, and I asked, "Could you help me?" The Iditarod didn't have much money, either, and they said no. I took out a loan to pay for the printing costs, and my first Iditarod poster came out in January 1977. It sold for five dollars. The print market was just taking hold with signed and numbered prints, and I wondered if it was OK to do that with a poster. We decided, yeah, it was because we said it was. There was a printing of twenty-five hundred, and one thousand were signed and numbered. The Iditarod bought them at half price, sold them at the full five dollars, and kept the profit.

I wanted to promote the Iditarod and what it stands for. For me, that is independence and toughness, setting a goal and accomplishing that goal. The dogs—and the type of dog, the husky—are part of that too.

There was never a plan for the poster to be an annual thing. That first year, I took the date off the picture in the printing process. We didn't know how fast they would sell and thought maybe they would be around for a couple of years. But the next year, the Iditarod came back around and said, "Can you do it again?" I asked them if they would loan me the money, and they said no.

It just went on from there. The twenty-eighth poster will be out for the 2004 race. Why am I still doing it? I still believe in what the race stands for. What it does is keep old-time values—what Alaska used to be—within us.

I have also been producing Iditarod prints since 1983. The public links me to the Iditarod. But the public being the way the public is, they know you for one thing. If you want to expand your career and be nationally and internationally known, then you have to get away from just that dog thing. I'd rather be known as an artist with a broader body of work. But this is meaningful to me. More than anything else.

A lot of people ask me which one of the posters is my favorite. I have to say the 1983 poster, the scene of a musher traveling under a dark sky on a full-moon night with the words "Alone on the Crest of Your Dreams" across the poster. I pick that one because of the title. In a lot of ways, that sums up the Iditarod.

In 1979 I raced in my second Iditarod. I knew about the trail. I knew where to stop and where not to stop. I also had ten thousand miles or more on my team. I trained them to be faster, but the dogs were going to go the speed they were going to go. They were Siberian huskies. That's what I've always had.

During the race, I was looking for things because I knew what I wanted to do when I came back. I wanted to paint it again. I was looking for the artistic experience. I did enjoy that race, but I could see the changes coming down the road. It was just starting to be a competitive thing as opposed to being an experience.

Also, I remember pulling into McGrath, and I don't ever remember having such back pains in my life as I had during that race. My back was killing me. I was OD-ing on aspirin. That contributed to my not doing the Iditarod again. I finished in forty-second place, completing the race about six days faster than I had in 1976.

After that, I got very happy doing short trips, just traveling, not having to prove myself again or prove my dogs. I still have eighteen dogs that I take on trips with my wife, Jona. We go fifty or a hundred miles. We attend the Iditarod pre-race banquet in Anchorage, and we talk about the Iditarod to kids in schools and to groups around the country and in Europe. The Iditarod is still very much a part of me.

[In March 2004, Jon Van Zyle was inducted into Iditarod Trail Sled Dog Race Hall of Fame.]

RACE RECORD

1982	17 days, 10 hours, 27 minutes	22nd
1995	11 days, 7 hours	20th
1996	10 days, 6 hours, 27 minutes	15th
1997	10 days, 14 hours, 31 minutes	16th
1998	9 days, 12 hours, 18 minutes	4th
1999	10 days, 14 hours, 26 minutes	11th
2000	9 days, 19 hours, 15 minutes	9th
2001	13 days, 7 hours, 56 minutes	42nd
2002	9 days, 14 hours, 25 minutes	11th
2003	10 days, 14 hours, 12 minutes	12th

CHAPTER 4
MITCH SEAVEY

Mushing and the Iditarod have long played a huge role in the lives of the Seavey clan of Seward, Alaska. Mitch, forty-four, is the primary racer in the family now, but his father, Dan, placed third in the inaugural Iditarod in 1973 and fifth in 1974. Mitch's sons Danny and Tyrell have also competed. In 2001 Mitch and Danny were joined on the trail in a comeback race by Dan, making the Seaveys the first to put three generations of the same family into the Iditarod in the same year.

For more than a decade the Seaveys have operated a mushing business that offers dogsled rides to tourists and have spread the gospel of the Iditarod to thousands of visitors. Mitch Seavey made  his Iditarod debut in 1982, then did not return to the race until 1995. He has become a regular competitor since.

My dad was my Iditarod influence, and my connection with the race began when I was about nine years old. I was a little kid tagging along when my dad and Joe Redington Sr. went fishing on the famous boat *Nomad.* The boat is now in derelict condition on the mud flats in Knik near Joe Redington's old homestead.

Actually, my dad met Tom Johnson, one of the Palmer teachers who helped Joe get the Iditarod started, when he first got to Alaska in 1963. They were both running dogs. My dad, Joe, and Tom talked about a long-distance race. They held that shorter Iditarod in 1967 for the Alaska Centennial, and we were in Louisiana because my dad was on sabbatical. But after we came back, he helped with the startup of the Iditarod we know today.

Being a history buff, and Alaska history being one of his subjects, Dad had a lot to do with the historical routing of the trail. I was thirteen or fourteen when the Iditarod started, and I helped train dogs. We'd hook up, and Dad would have ten and I'd have three. We did a lot of training outside of Seward, over near Sterling and Skilak Road—some of the same trails where I still train.

Dad ran the first Iditarod and finished third. There were a lot of stories about how much trouble Joe had raising the $50,000 purse. Since Dad was one of the few top finishers with a steady job, Joe asked if he could borrow the $6,000 prize back. Eventually, the Iditarod Trail Committee paid Dad back with interest.

When Dad ran in the first one, there was a question of whether the mushers would even make it. They were treated as heroes because they finished the race. It seemed like it didn't matter as much whether you were first, tenth, or twentieth. There was a really neat atmosphere, and it electrified me.

Even though I was only about fourteen, I felt that I would run the Iditarod someday. You know kids with their imagination. I'd be running along the road near our house where we mushed the dogs, always imagining I was on the Iditarod, finishing the race or winning the race, even though I was only running four dogs.

I got the chance to run the Iditarod for the first time in 1982, and my son Danny was born two months after the race. All of the kids—my wife, Janine, and I have four boys—have helped with the kennel and the chores the way I helped my dad. I'm really pleased with that. In our family, doing chores, being responsible, and doing your work is not really optional. We have dogs, kids have chores, they take care of the dogs. But racing or even running the dogs in training, that has always been something they wanted to do.

They have always been extremely excited to run the Junior Iditarod or the Iditarod. It's a lot of fun to see that they've done the work—the drudgery—for most of their lives, and still love the dogs and love the sport. Now Danny and Tyrell are both attending the University of Montana.

I don't know if they will ever come back to dogs, and I don't particularly care, but I think it's excellent for them to have worked with the dogs and raced. We've home-schooled the kids and we have our own way of doing things, but it almost seems as if running the Iditarod has turned into a rite of passage. Once you've done the Iditarod, you're on your own.

The boys have worked and helped me get ready for all of these races, and now they run the race and see what it's like. They see the trail. Then they have that in the bank and they go on. If they ever want to come back to it, they kind of know what it is.

When my dad and Danny and I went together in 2001, that was exciting. Any time you put three teams in a race, it is a tremendous amount of work. It has its drawbacks, but that year it was a lot of fun with three generations of Seaveys in the race. Three in one family in the same race made training difficult, though. I was going to be the competitive one, and my team was undertrained. As it turned out, I held up in Grayling and waited for my dad and Danny to catch up. We ran the rest of the race together. Although I was disappointed from a competitive point of view, it was one of the best times I've ever had on the Iditarod. I finished forty-second, Danny was forty-third, and my dad was forty-fourth.

In 2003 we had three teams going again. Dallas was running the Junior Iditarod. Tyrell and I were in the Iditarod. That gave me a second son as an Iditarod rookie.

My rookie year was 1982, and I probably have more memories from that race than from any other single race. As a rookie I had a lot of apprehensions, and that was a tough training year. We live on the coast, so no-snow years are not new to us. That year we ended up traveling all the way to Nenana, near Fairbanks, to train. Then,

I think the day the Iditarod began, it started snowing and didn't stop until we were in Nome. The race took me more than seventeen days. My best time now is about 9½ days.

Even as a rookie, I was running the race to be competitive. It never occurred to me to just kind of camp along. I was as high as fifth place in McGrath. Different things happened. Out of Unalakleet, about eleven miles from Shaktoolik on the flats, I got in one of those instant ground storms. That pretty well stopped several of us. We just got pinned down, and I believe I was there for forty-eight hours.

People thought I was lost because I was out there in the weather so long. I tried to backtrack into some timber to get a little bit out of the wind. I fed my dogs, and my plan was to just get into my sleeping bag and wait it out. I was half in, and I didn't have my mitts on. Joe Redington came along and woke me up. My hands got pretty frozen. I was not in danger of losing any fingers, but I did lose feeling in the fingers on both hands. They've never been the same since.

My hands get cold pretty easily, and kind of numb. I've always been thankful that Joe came along. He waited for me to get my tug lines hooked up on the dogs. We were going to try to go together. The weather was still brutal. It was probably blowing seventy knots, about zero degrees, and we got turned back again.

This time we went farther back into the trees and camped. I felt OK about it since Joe couldn't go either; I wasn't just wimping out. A couple of other guys were there too. A dozen or so teams had made it to Shaktoolik, and the race was trying to bring food in from Unalakleet by snowmachine. When they passed us, we raided the food supplies and were able to take care of our dogs.

Later the second day, I just got tired of being stuck there and decided I was going to Shaktoolik. We got out on the ice and it was the same deal again. Couldn't go, couldn't go. My dogs wanted to, and then it got so windy that they wanted to turn around. They got all twisted up. I ended up hooking a line to the front of the leader and just walking. I probably walked halfway to Shaktoolik before it got dark.

In those days we didn't have reflective markers to help us see at night, and it got darker and darker in whiteout conditions. I couldn't see the markers anymore, so I tied my team to the last marker I could find and stayed until daylight.

I climbed into my sled, but first I had to take some stuff out. I pulled a small nylon tarp out of the sled, and the wind caught it and just yanked it out of my hands and it flew away. Then nearly the same thing happened to my sleeping bag, which was really frightening. The wind was trying to take it from my hands, and it was with one last grasp that I got hold of the bag.

I got the sleeping bag shoved down into my sled bag and crawled in. Most people had down bags. But my sister, Tracie Audette, worked at Gary King's Sporting Goods in Anchorage, and she had shown up at the starting line with one of those newfangled synthetic bags. Since she'd gone to all of that trouble, I switched bags. Well, as it turns out, it may have saved my life.

I shivered throughout the night. Everything was soaked from snow blowing in. The Bering Sea coast snow is just like flour, and it blows through the pores and fibers of your clothing and gear. My sled bag was packed with this snow. Had I not had the synthetic sleeping bag, I would have been really cold. In the morning the wind was down to twenty or thirty knots and we drove into Shaktoolik. I was kind of a wide-eyed rookie, and the whole thing was a little overwhelming.

When I ran that Iditarod, I thought it might be the only time I ever did it. I was involved with the church and we had kids, and then in 1986 we moved to Virginia. We became partners with Janine's brother and a cousin in real estate development. We stayed there for six years, working in real estate and home building. I wasn't there long before I realized I wanted to come back to Alaska.

I think I had to go away to realize how much I missed it. The contrast solidified the decision for me. Now I'm very comfortable doing what I'm doing, and I don't feel that I'm missing something. From that standpoint, I wish the same for my kids. If they ever come back to dogs, they'll have some other perspective to see if it's what they really want to do.

I got back to Alaska in 1992, but I didn't do the Iditarod again until 1995. My dad had a few dogs, but they weren't prime Iditarod dogs; they were his recreational dogs. We started building a team. In 1993 and 1994 I ran the Copper Basin 300. In 1995 I did the Iditarod, and I've done every Iditarod since. When I came back, I pulled off a twentieth place. I was trying to be competitive. I wasn't in there just to see the trail.

In 1998 I finished fourth and had a fast time: 9 days, 12 hours, 18 minutes. I had a lot of young dogs. I started out thinking that I hadn't run so many two-year-olds before and that these guys were going to be a bit soft. I thought I would have to take it easy, and it worked out that a conservative start seemed to develop a real strong team later. I passed a lot of teams, and then we hit a storm. Once you get into a storm everything slows down, and even if your team is faster, you can't really make up a lot of time. We just kind of trudged along in position.

I had been in Shaktoolik for a couple of hours when DeeDee Jonrowe and Jeff King left. I was watching them and thinking, Oh, there goes the front of the race. It never occurred to me to give chase, or change my schedule, or attempt to catch up with them. I was just glad to be where I was. It was the most competitive I had been, but I was totally relaxed and non-competitive about it other than wanting to be in the top ten.

Those two-year-olds turned out to be the best dogs I've ever had. They've been in my team every year, and they're remarkable dogs. Those type of dogs come along only once in a while, and they make a big difference.

I made some good moves early in the race. It was a warm year. I got into good position and moved along, but I got into Nikolai and the temperature was in the thirties. I had planned to take my twenty-four-hour layover in McGrath, and when I left Nikolai it was about noon in the warm weather. It was kind of a risky move. But my dogs did really well going to McGrath. I stopped quite a bit. I let them play in the snow. I talked to them. I kept them happy, and we made a reasonable run. So I was in McGrath, already on my twenty-four, and most of my competitors were still in Nikolai waiting for the weather to cool down. In hindsight, if I had made one more jump to Takotna and then started my twenty-four, I would have had something going.

Later, I got a little off my schedule at Nulato because I broke my sled. How do you break a sled on the Yukon River? There was a place where the ice had settled, so it was at an angle. I was going over it and slid down and hit something solid sideways and broke all the stanchions on one side of my sled.

I hadn't planned to stop in Nulato. Then I had one of my most miserable runs ever, from Nulato to Kaltag, again in warm weather. The wind was blowing about ten miles an hour behind us and we were moving about ten miles an hour, so we were traveling in absolute calm. It was sunny and hot; that made it a hard, hard run. All of the leaders were in Kaltag, and I stayed about 2½ hours.

I was going to gobble them up if I could. I still had twelve dogs; I felt my team was strong, and I had been resting them. It was like having money in the bank. I had never run them longer than six hours at a time. Instead of running all the way from Unalakleet to Kaltag, I stopped at Old Woman cabin and gave them a two-hour rest. I didn't want to make a ten- or eleven-hour nonstop run. But after that, I was on a mission.

When I went through Unalakleet, I passed people. On the run to Shaktoolik, I passed people. Between there and Koyuk, I passed a bunch of teams. I passed Doug Swingley and Martin Buser. Charlie Boulding stuck with me, and we ended up spending the rest of the race together. Still, I always felt that DeeDee and Jeff were gone. Charlie and I might have caught DeeDee if we had paid more attention to the times between checkpoints. But we stayed an extra two hours at White Mountain because of the storm, and from White Mountain to Safety we were goofing around and feeding our dogs. The nearest competitor was John Baker, nine hours behind us, so we had no urgency.

Charlie and I basically knew we were going to have to race at some point. As it worked out, Charlie had very tough dogs, and as the storm developed and the trail deteriorated, it got more and more difficult. He had better leaders for those conditions; I followed Charlie into Safety and never made an effort to pass him.

He was breaking most of the trail from White Mountain to Safety. Then I stopped to make some adjustments, and he got a gap on me. He beat me into Nome by thirty-seven minutes, but I was happy with fourth.

Coming in fourth was very much a step up. But it was only my fifth Iditarod, and I didn't have a lot of the depth of experience I needed. This whole thing is not just a race. It's a breeding program, and what you do with your feeding program, and how you train, and how lucky you get with the weather. There's so much to it.

I think the fourth-place finish actually set me up to make mistakes in the future, because I was overly confident and didn't know what got me to fourth position. But tiny changes can have tremendous effects later in the race. Even changes in training. Living on the Kenai Peninsula, we might have the best conditions one year while others are struggling with snow, and then we might have rain and ice, and no snow.

I don't plan on stopping my Iditarod racing until I win. I have a lot of confidence that as hard as we work—and we make a study out of it with my family helping me—that it will happen. I have the utmost respect for the people who have won this race. Most of them are my friends. I don't have any rivals or enemies. They're all people who I can sit down with and have coffee. They train dogs. They have families. They have dogs that get lame. They have sleds that break. All the same things happen. There's nothing magical. They're not any smarter, or better, or gifted. So we'll have our day.

I keep learning. I make mistakes. I'm not ashamed of that. You learn by experience. We only get to do this once a year. We do it, and then it seems like forever until we race again. In wrestling, which I did in high school, we would have ten matches in two weekends. It takes a long time to find out about dogs. You breed them and you don't really know how good they are until they're at least three. If that was a mistake, you've wasted that time. If that was the right thing to do and you go back and repeat it in enough numbers to shape your team, it takes six years. You really have to commit.

My family is a big thread in my Iditarod racing. Our sled dog business, Iditarides Sled Dog Tours, is not just about the Iditarod, but we're an Iditarod family, and that's a big part of it. Winning the race would be nice, but to me Iditarod is a part of life and it reflects on your whole life. How you conduct yourself as you go about your enterprise speaks a lot about you and your character.

One thing we get out of the Iditarod, even more so than winning, is a format to raise kids. Character issues are developed differently today than they were a hundred years ago. You have to be in some specialty like the Iditarod to learn responsibility and dedication, and to have the opportunity to test your character. I wouldn't want to raise my kids on video games—they do have video games, but they don't have time to play them.

When my kids are fourteen or fifteen, I look at them more as adults. We depend on them for things. If I had to look for somebody to handle a bad situation, I would look to any one of my three older kids. My youngest is six.

I expect a lot from them, and they do it. I don't baby them, but we have a very loving, fun time. We hug a lot. We're running fourteen dogs eighty miles a day. That's not a big deal to them. Cleaning the yard for 120 dogs, building a chain-link fence—I'll get them started, but I expect them to do it. "I can't" isn't part of the vocabulary around here.

As a person, I'm very absolute; I see things in black and white. The fence is either done or it isn't done. I don't let my kids tell me they couldn't finish or that they ran out of something. I tell them to go get whatever they need, because they're not done yet. It's like the old farm environment of rural America, and a lot of our country was that way a hundred years ago. Most kids knew how to plow with horses when they were twelve, and how to repair a wagon wheel, and how to help a cow give birth. Now parents are lucky if they can get kids seventeen or eighteen to clean their own rooms.

On our tour business we have two carts; each one can carry seven adults for about two miles. We use twelve dogs and have five tour times a day. We handle thousands of people in a four-month summer. I think our record is 170 people in a day. We've hired my kids and their friends—other teenagers who are of the same ilk—to give the rides. They do an awesome job.

We talk about the Iditarod and the Iditarod Trail, which starts in Seward, so we have the local connection. People know the Iditarod. They are just fascinated by it. It's been an upward curve in the ten years we've been running tours. Taking a sled-dog ride in the summer has gone from "you've got to be kidding" to what tourists expect to do.

I haven't been giving the tours myself the last couple of years. We have 150 dogs—we can justify that number simply because we rotate them—and only keep 75 in Seward. We always have fresh, eager, happy dogs to do the tours. That's what we want the tourists to see.

I think I'll race the Iditarod for a long time, although there are times when it's difficult because I have to go look for snow. During the winter of 2002–2003, being away from home was the most difficult thing for me. I lived at the Wolverine Lodge, away from home, for most of the winter.

Not only is being away an expense, but I also have a six-year-old kid, Conway, who cries when I leave. He calls me up and cries and says, "Why do you have to do the Iditarod?" It has crossed my mind to take a break until he's bigger. You can be in your fifties and sixties and be smart enough to compensate for slowing down.

I don't need to do this. If I never win the Iditarod, it won't change me as a person. If I win, it won't change me as a person. I am who I am, and I'm happy with that. But that's the goal, and you have to have a goal, or what do you do, go in circles?

RACE RECORD

1982	16 days, 14 hours, 54 minutes	13th
1984	12 days, 15 hours, 7 minutes	1st
2003	Scratched	

CHAPTER 5
DEAN OSMAR

Dean Osmar, fifty-seven, of Coho, Alaska, was an Iditarod phantom. Osmar finished thirteenth in the Iditarod in 1982, won in 1984, and then disappeared into the mists, not racing again until 2003. The combination of the victory and then bowing out of the race in favor of son Tim gave Dean Osmar a legendary mystique. He actually compares the scenario to J. D. Salinger, author of his favorite book, *The Catcher in the Rye*, who essentially became a recluse.

The Osmars are long-time Alaskans. Dean's father, Per, who was born in Sweden, homesteaded in Alaska in the 1940s. They became commercial fishermen. Fishing was a summertime occupation, and in the late 1960s Osmar's family spent winters in Billings, Montana. There, in his teens, he became a Golden Gloves boxer.

The family's mushing lineage began in the 1950s, when Per Osmar helped a neighbor check his trapline. In 1979 Dean obtained his first puppies from early Iditarod musher Rod Perry by trading an old wooden dory with a value of $600 for three dogs.

Dean Osmar was obsessed with participating in the Iditarod and winning it. When he succeeded so quickly, Osmar lost some of his racing fire. Over the years, Osmar has occasionally employed other mushers, such as Paul Gebhardt and Iditarod champion Martin Buser, on his commercial fishing crews.

In 1982 I was glad to finally be entered in the Iditarod. But I almost didn't get to go. I ruptured my appendix on January 12 and just about died. I was training dogs. My wife rushed me to the hospital in Soldotna, and the surgeon wasn't there. It took them seven hours to round up a surgeon.

By the time they got me under the knife, the appendix was so inflamed that they weren't sure I was going to make it. I ended up spending ten days in the hospital, and had three different kinds of antibiotics and IVs and all of that stuff. My weight dropped from 178 pounds to 139 pounds in about two weeks.

I couldn't train anymore up until the race, so Timmy—he was just a kid—ended up training the dogs. He was probably about sixteen then. A friend of ours, Alan Perry, helped. I could hardly stand up.

About a week before the race, I took my first run. Every time the handlebar hit my stomach, it felt like knives going in there. I figured I would try it, and I figured I'd go for a few days and drop out if I just couldn't do it. I took off from the starting line pretty weak.

It was not a fun way to do the Iditarod. I was feeling sort of wimpy, and a lot of teams passed me. Norman Vaughan—he was in his seventies then—and I traveled together. Norman, who ended up scratching, said, "I believe I can get by you," and passed me going into Skwentna.

I called Tim on the phone because my stomach hurt and I was weak, and the dogs weren't running very well. I told him I was going to drop out, and he acted like he didn't hear me. He said, "Just go on into the next checkpoint and see how you feel." I did that, and I felt a little stronger. At the next checkpoint I felt a little stronger. Between Nikolai and McGrath, I started feeling pretty good. I ran into Susan Butcher and Rick Swenson, who had been leading the race, and that was a shock. I didn't realize I was anywhere close to them.

My team was young and it was slow, but I was leaving checkpoints maybe an hour and a half before Susan and Rick and Jerry Austin and that bunch. They'd all catch me and beat me into the next checkpoint by an hour. They were getting five hours rest, and

I was getting about three. I got into the lead after Ruby and led seven of the last ten checkpoints.

I was eating about five thousand calories a day and building my strength. I was starving. When I got to Shaktoolik, I stopped for two days because a storm was blowing about sixty miles an hour. The wind was so powerful it would blow me over. I couldn't leave.

We made it to White Mountain, but just barely. It was a total whiteout. I knew I wasn't going to win, but I did want to be rookie of the year. We rested four or five hours. When I pulled out, it was right behind a group of about seven. Everybody passed me.

Then it got pretty scary. It was a nighttime whiteout, and I had no clue where I was. I kept getting off the trail. Finally, we were more off the trail than on it. I'd run up with the leaders and drag them a little, trying to find the trail. But I couldn't find it. I should have just jumped into the sleeping bag right then, but I thought I'd be smart. I set the hook and looked for trail markers.

I walked to the front of the team first, then I kept walking right and left looking for trail markers. I knew I wasn't far from the trail, but I couldn't find the markers. And then I couldn't find my way back to the team.

I knew I was finished if I couldn't make it back. I was weak, the temperature was thirty below zero, and the wind was blowing about forty miles an hour. The snow was knee-deep, and the wind was just howling and blowing. I figured I was screwed. There was no shelter, no way to build a fire. I had no food or water. Everything was at the sled.

I started walking in circles, really tight circles. Then I expanded them to bigger and bigger circles. Finally, when I was damned near exhausted and getting hypothermic, I actually tripped over the gang line. I didn't even see the dogs. I was between the third pair of dogs, and I pulled my way back to the sled.

I tipped the sled over, got the sleeping bag out, and crawled into it wearing my bunny boots and parka and everything. I was shivering so badly that I couldn't take them off. But I had a thermos full of really hot chocolate, about two quarts. I drank that and ate about a pound of cashews. I fell asleep, and my body heat came back. I stayed three or four hours. Nobody came by. When it got to be daylight, I shook off the snow and I was feeling pretty good.

In the light I could see a trail marker about 150 yards away. A couple of teams had gone by and didn't even know I was there. That's the closest I've come to dying on the trail. I felt pretty lucky.

We got back on the trail and back in the race, but I got passed by several other mushers within seven or eight miles of Nome and finished in thirteenth place. I was pretty slow going from Safety to Nome. I wasn't even rookie of the year. Stan Zuray beat me. He was ninth. But given the circumstances of maybe not even starting the race, it was OK. I gained some confidence. I also knew a lot of those mushers had adult teams and I was running pups.

When I got to thinking about it in Nome, I decided it was a hell of an accomplishment. It's a hell of an accomplishment nowadays just to finish, even if a guy is toward the back of the pack.

I actually gained six pounds during the 1982 race. Mushers usually lose about sixteen pounds along the trail. My body was just craving calories. I felt stronger at the end than I did at the start. I came into Nome around midnight, and we danced until six o'clock in the morning.

Once I finished the Iditarod, I knew I would do it until I won it. That was my goal. I didn't feel I had the team to win in 1983. I didn't think the dogs were old enough. So I did a lot of middle distance racing. And Tim won the Junior Iditarod. We pooled our dogs back then.

It was a good feeling, going into training for the 1983–84 season. I felt I was sneaking up on people a little. The top mushers knew who I was from 1982. They nicknamed me "The Trailbreaker." They used me to set the pace, which was fine with them. I don't think they paid attention to me as someone who they thought might beat them. It was a big help.

We took off in the middle of the pack. The weather was warm, thirty-three degrees above zero. It was raining, and there was deep snow on the trail. It was a warm year, and that's what I wanted. I didn't have the speed in my team that a lot of the other mushers had. But I had the power and the toughness. I trained in warmer weather than the Fairbanks boys did, and, of course, Rick Swenson and Susan Butcher were the two main ones I worried about. On the second day, I passed Swenson and he was a little grumpy. Then I passed Butcher and she was a little grumpy.

I think I was second into Rainy Pass, first into Rohn River, and first into McGrath, and I just never looked back. I got a heck of a big break at Rohn River when the others declared their twenty-four-hour rest. It was wet and miserable, and it was starting to freeze. The snow was starting to get a bit crusty.

Swenson thought that if he stayed for twenty-four hours and the trail froze, it would be terrible for the dogs' feet. So he pulled the hook and left after about nine hours. I was almost ten hours into my layover. I didn't dare leave. Joe Garnie and I just shook our heads and wondered what those guys were doing, forfeiting all of that time. Most of the other good guys left, except Joe Redington Sr. Joe Garnie and I couldn't believe how much of a gift it was.

Then it warmed up, and the trail wasn't bad on the dogs' feet. In Nikolai, all of the others were sleeping. After McGrath, the only teams I saw were Joe Redington and Joe Garnie. Joe Garnie raced to all of the checkpoints. At the halfway point in Cripple, I did rest eleven hours, and Butcher, Swenson, and all the rest of the guys caught me. But I was going out when Susan was coming in. I think a lot of them thought they had caught me and weren't too worried about me. They were still worried about beating Swenson. He had won four times since 1977.

But Swenson had a slower team that year. He just didn't have the great team he usually had. I saw Joe Garnie in Galena, and he left at the same time I did, but I never saw anybody again. I think when the others reached Kaltag, they realized Swenson wasn't a threat, that it was probably me. They started pushing hard, but it was a little too late. When I left Unalakleet, Susan was about eight hours behind me, and I only beat her by an hour and thirty minutes. In one more day she would have caught me.

It didn't help that I got lost around Moses Point going into

Elim. I went off on a trapline trail. I lost about three hours. It was a trail that paralleled the other trail for a while and then veered off. I never did yell or scream or get too upset, because I knew that would screw up the dogs. They pick up on your problems. So I kept really calm and acted like I knew what I was doing.

One more place I almost lost the race was Golovin. A big tide had come in, and it was starting to freeze up. As I crossed Golovin Bay, there were maybe 2½ inches of ice on top of maybe 1½ feet of water. Every third step, we'd fall through. The trail markers were all down. The tide had washed in, and they had been tipped over. It took me 1½ hours more than it should have to get to White Mountain. I was making only three miles an hour, walking with the leaders, switching leaders, scaring the hell out of the dogs as they fell through the top layer.

In White Mountain I was pretty well beat-up, and the dogs were pretty well beat-up. I was just hoping we could stay four hours and not see anybody come in. What I didn't know was that when Susan and Joe Garnie came by a few hours later, it had frozen solid, so they just whipped right across. They could see the spots where we had fallen through.

I was still cautiously optimistic when we left White Mountain. I knew I had a lead of at least four hours, but I didn't know if it was four hours and ten minutes, or nine hours. The dogs were groggy at first, but after a little while they started moving well. And it was a beautiful day.

I stopped, and I was snacking the dogs and feeling pretty smart when some guys came up on a snowmachine. They gave me some misinformation. They made coffee and sandwiches and wanted me to take a while talking to them. I said I had to get going because I was worried Susan was going to catch me. They said not to worry about her, that she and Joe Garnie had given up the chase.

Figuring I had it made, I stopped with them for about twenty-five minutes. Then they brought out some whiskey and I thought, Nah, I'd better get going. When I got to Safety, Tim was there. He had flown in. I said I was going to stop and have some moose stew. He said, "What are you doing? You probably don't have that big a lead. Maybe you want to get going."

I wanted that moose stew. I was pretty darned hungry, and those snowmachiners had told me Susan was way back. Tim said,

"No, there are a couple of teams not too far behind you." I pulled the hook and left Safety. I ate some of the stew between Safety and Nome. By then it was nighttime, and there weren't too many markers. Every time I thought I might be off the trail, I stopped the dogs and walked ahead to find the next marker. I was moving fast, but I was stopping to make damned sure I wasn't off the trail.

Then I looked behind me and saw lights. I figured, Oh hell, they've caught me. But they were from snowmachines, not mushers' headlamps. I got nervous, though. You just never know until you get underneath the arch on Front Street.

I got in at midnight. It was unbelievable. There were so many people. I finished in 12 days, 15 hours, 7 minutes. Susan was 1½ hours behind me, and Garnie was 37 minutes behind her. They had a car out there with flashing lights leading me in. I had a feeling of exhilaration. I had been obsessed with the Iditarod, and I had achieved a goal.

We partied until six in the morning again. I danced with a lot of girls. The winner gets to dance with all of the pretty girls. I was pretty hot stuff at the Board of Trade. They had the biggest party.

Afterward, Swenson congratulated me and apologized for being a little grumpy on the trail. We became good friends after that. And I became good friends with Joe Garnie. It was a helluva night, a very big night. Susan congratulated me. Several mushers asked where I had come from and how I had pulled it off. Terry Adkins and Jerry Austin were pretty jazzed about it. The public was glad for me. I was a new face. I made a lot of friends along the trail in the Athabascan and Eskimo villages, friends I still have to this day.

I announced right then and there at the finish line when they gave me the microphone that I wasn't going to race again. I said that Tim would probably have some of the same dogs the next year, and he did. I still raced dogs, and I raced every year after that, but nothing like the Iditarod.

Then, in 2003, I decided to do the Iditarod again, for different reasons. I wanted to travel with my group of two-year-olds to make a trip out of it. And my best friend died. He was a big friend of the Iditarod. He had sled dogs and trapline dogs, and I did it to honor his memory and to visit old friends along the trail. My attitude was, if I came in first, great; if I came in fifty-first, great.

Trying to win the Iditarod again is definitely a two- or three-year plan. I knew I was not going to win it the first year back after being gone nineteen years. I've got forty-four dogs, more than I ever had in my life.

Timmy and I talked about my doing the Yukon Quest, or just taking a thousand-mile trip someplace in Alaska. There would be some neat places to go. A guy could go across the Brooks Range and up to the North Slope. One of my goals would be to go to Yellowknife in the Northwest Territories and mush to Baffin Island, spending about two months on a two-thousand-mile trip.

Whenever I sat around talking with mushers, having a cup of coffee or a beer, they always asked if I might do it again. Back when I said I was finished with the Iditarod right after winning, they didn't believe it. Even Timmy didn't believe it.

Newcomers come along, and they look in the history books and say, "Who is that old guy?" People who are big fans of the race still come up to me whenever I go to Fairbanks or Anchorage. The real Iditarod fans know who all of the champions are, even if they've been out of sight.

The race has gotten so much faster since I won, and the trail is marked better. The first one out always has a perfectly marked trail that favors a fast runner. But even at its best, with a good trail and good markings and good weather, the Iditarod is still a very hard thing to do. There are a lot of people who are never going to make it.

RACE RECORD

1973	Scratched	
1974	23 days, 1 hour, 55 minutes	7th
1985	20 days, 3 hours, 38 minutes	19th
1986	15 days, 7 hours, 12 minutes	29th
1987	Scratched	
1990	15 days, 5 hours, 37 minutes	32nd
1991	16 days, 10 hours, 2 minutes	29th
1997	11 days, 18 hours	25th
1998	11 days, 9 hours, 31 minutes	26th
1999	12 days, 19 hours, 25 minutes	32nd
2000	11 days, 22 minutes	9th
2001	12 days, 18 hours, 14 minutes	34th

CHAPTER 6
RAYMIE REDINGTON

Raymie Redington, fifty-nine, of Knik, Alaska, is a member of the most famous family in long-distance mushing. His dad, Joe Redington Sr., was known as the Father of the Iditarod, and several members of his family have competed. Recently, Raymie's son Ray Jr. moved to the forefront of the next generation of Iditarod contenders.

Raymie competed in the first Iditarod in 1973 as a last-minute substitute for his father, who turned over the trained team. Raymie has been around dogs his whole life, and operates his kennel in Knik down the street from where his late father homesteaded and raised his own dogs.

Redington now runs dogsled trips for tourists at Iditarod Headquarters in Wasilla in the summer. Long before there was an Iditarod, Redington raced in the Fur Rendezvous World Championship sprint races in Anchorage. A student of mushing history, Redington collects items that harken back to the early days of mushing in Alaska and the early days of the Iditarod.

In 1973 my dad was working on getting the Iditarod started. Just before the race, he decided he had better stay behind and work on fundraising. He wanted me to take his dogs from Anchorage to Knik, but I kind of liked the way it was going, so I wanted to go all the way to Nome.

It was very cold during the race that year, and I quit in Galena. I've always wished I had never done that, but I didn't know much about racing. It was very cold—forty, fifty below— and there were no trails like we have today and no trail markers. Once in a while I found a broken limb on a tree. In one place, someone left an empty whiskey bottle. That was a trail marker.

I came back and did it in 1974 and placed seventh. I thought that was pretty good. In a race that long, you're always going to have problems. Even today, you're going to have ups and downs. It was just easier to have problems in 1973 and 1974. There were only three places we could drop dogs: McGrath, Galena, and Un-alakleet. Nowadays we can drop them at checkpoints everywhere; that makes it easier instead of packing them for miles and miles. It's better for the dogs too.

Back when my dad was starting the race, a lot of people doubted that someone could take a dog team a thousand miles. I was thinking that maybe they were right. I didn't say it around my dad. It was tough, and we didn't know how far we were going to go in a day. One of those years, I was with Dick Mackey on the Salmon River and it snowed three feet. We camped at forty-eight below. Dick had a bottle of whiskey that a guy had given him, and it had slush in it. There was no trail and there were no snowmachines to break trail. We had to snowshoe and look for the trail. It was just altogether different than it is today. After I quit in Galena in 1973, I wanted to get to Nome in 1974. Then I didn't race until 1985.

It was fifty below when I got to Galena, and I was down to seven or eight dogs. I think I was in about fifth or sixth place, but I just kind of got burned out. Later, I wished I'd never quit. I just didn't know what was ahead. If I did, I would have known that I could get dog food and everything in the villages.

In 1974 I said, "I'm gonna make it this time." It was nice running with my dad and Jerry Riley and the other guys. Even today, people finish the race and swear they're never going back, but a month later they can't wait to do it again because it's such a challenge. If you go just to have a good time, you won't want to keep doing it. It's the deals you go through, everything together, that make it.

I went fourteen times and always enjoyed it. Now I've got my boy, Ray, doing it, so I'll probably run it again. I might do the Yukon Quest for my dad. He wanted to do it before he passed away. Maybe for him, I'll try it. A Redington has never run it. My dad ran the Iditarod at eighty, so I know I can do it. If I can do it at sixty, I'll be pretty happy.

I'm going to be different than Dad was. When I'm eighty, if I'm alive, I going to be sitting in Hawaii. I won't be going down the Iditarod Trail. Actually, I won't leave Alaska, but if I have the choice at eighty, I'll be on vacation in Hawaii.

The trail is better nowadays, much smoother, but I had a guy ask me a couple of years ago, when it was rougher, "How did your dad ever hang on at eighty years old, going over them bumps and stuff?"

When everybody got to Nome in 1973 and proved it could be done, there was a lot of excitement. Alaska didn't have a snowmachine race, and a boat race, and all kinds of basketball teams. So it was a really big deal. It started to become real big in the villages. They'd pick names of mushers to stay with them. The race is bigger now—I never thought it would get so big—but it's just another thing to do.

The Iditarod is bigger around the world, though. I do tourist rides for the Iditarod, and a few years ago I did twenty-eight rides in a day. Now it's up over two hundred.

In the 1974 race, we started in Anchorage and went straight through to Nome. We didn't truck the dogs anywhere for a restart. I'm glad I was one of the old-timers who did that. I don't know if we could even do that today because of the traffic on the Glenn Highway and the Parks Highway.

I was in first place in McGrath, but I finished seventh because I lost a whole day on the trail. I made a wrong turn out of McGrath, went out on a trapline trail instead of the Iditarod Trail. I left at six in the morning and got back to McGrath at nine-thirty that night. An airplane met me, and the pilot told me I had done the wrong trail. I thought I would hit the Iditarod Trail eventually, but I kept going and going and going. Then I had to go all the way back and rest my dogs the next day. It really messed me up. I had a good team. But I was way behind after that.

Back then, we took more time talking to other mushers. We weren't in as big a hurry. I had a lot of good times. I went eight times with my dad. We saw a lot of good people. Iditarod mushers are mostly real nice people. Once you get out there and see how it is, I think the Iditarod makes you a better person.

I think you spend a lot of time thinking about family and what you're going to do when you get back, and what you're going to work on. I'm not sure if the dogs are any better today, but back then everybody seemed closer together and we would stay longer together in the checkpoints. In 1974 there were three Redingtons out there; my brother Joee raced, too, and he finished ninth.

In 2001 my boys Ray Jr. and Ryan and I all went out together, so there were three Redingtons again. It got me thinking about my dad and brother. I've been with all of the Redingtons on the trail. There was only one year when there weren't any Redingtons in the race, and my dad felt bad about that.

I was in the lead when I left McGrath in 1974. I had been running with Carl Huntington and he won. I still had a good time, even getting lost, but it was frustrating. It hurt. Today the trail is marked better.

I took a break from the Iditarod and came back in 1985. I was racing well again, and I got lost again. I finished nineteenth. Burt Bomhoff and John Barron and I all got lost in a storm on the ice going to Koyuk. We got lost for a long time, man. We left Shaktoolik, and we couldn't see. We waited for a long time before we went out, and we thought it was getting better and we left. That was a nice team. I was in the lead in Shageluk.

The wind was blowing; it was something else. When we stopped and the dogs curled up, they were covered with snow. When we went out, our dogs kept turning to the right. The wind was blowing hard in their faces, and they just kept turning out on the sea ice. Then we couldn't go any more. We turned the teams around, anchored the sleds, and jumped into the sled bags. It was cold. I think we stopped for over a day.

A snowmachine came out and found us. It was getting rough. It was getting wet. We couldn't go anywhere. We couldn't see anything. Later, when I did the Iditarod again, people would say, "Don't go with him. You'll get cold weather. You'll get lost." Because I got lost twice.

I did the Iditarod three years in a row in the 1980s, and then I took three years off. I knew I was going to come back, though. I never got rid of my dogs. I have over one hundred dogs now. I've got nice dogs now, probably the best I ever had. Everybody has the best they ever had. I don't know if the dogs are any better than they used to be, but there are more of them. A lot of guys raise them. Everybody's got a lot of dogs.

The way things have been going, with Doug Swingley and Martin Buser and Jeff King winning all the time, I think the public would like a new winner. Maybe another Alaskan, Ramy Brooks or John Baker. They've both been up there. Some people complained about Swingley because he came from Montana, but he always speaks well of my dad. I like Swingley. I think he was good for the race. But people were getting tired of the same guys winning. It's like basketball, where the Lakers were always winning. Instead of watching the game on TV, people would go outside to play basketball because they knew the Lakers were going to win.

I'd like to see an Alaska Native win the Iditarod. People in Alaska would be more into it. It's an Alaska deal, and naturally they want to see an Alaskan win it. Maybe the guy from Norway [Robert Sorlie] will come in and win it, and fans will be begging Swingley to get in and bring it back to the United States. [Robert Sorlie won the Iditarod in 2003.]

I don't think there's a much bigger symbol of Alaska than the Iditarod. I get people from Georgia; I get people from South Carolina, from North Carolina, to watch me race. Eight of them flew to Nome one time just to watch. Iditarod brings the state a lot of money.

I'm into old mushers, and I've got some pictures and stuff. I think about them all the time, how they got into it and how they stayed in it. I like the history. I think we're still connected to the old All-Alaska Sweepstakes, and that was before 1920.

People are interested in dogs. In 2002 I gave over eight thousand rides to tourists between May and September at Iditarod Headquarters. I never had one person who didn't like it. It's only about an eighth of a mile, just a circle, riding behind ten dogs, so it's good power. They can't believe how well trained the dogs are and how they go by voice commands. The ride only lasts about three or four minutes, but they can see how the dogs work together. It costs five dollars a ride. I do more grown-ups than I do kids. I've done it six years.

I tell them a little bit about the Iditarod, and I let them touch the dogs. They can't believe how friendly they are. Iditarod dogs are not mean. We've got people working on their feet and veterinarians messing around with them, and I've never heard of one of them biting. If you breed them right, they don't fight. There's no biting, no violence in them at all.

The tourists come from every state and from foreign countries. I get 'em from everywhere. I've had a lot from South Africa. A lot of people don't understand the Iditarod, and they're against it. They've got to come and check it out and see what we're doing. More and more people like the Iditarod. They see movies like *Iron Will* and *Snow Dogs,* and that kind of helps the race. Of course, they think the real Iditarod is like the cinema Iditarod.

I'm glad to be a Redington. I'm proud of my dad for getting the race going. I'm proud of my brothers. I'm proud of my son racing the race and everybody who's involved with dogs. I'll tell you one thing: Most kids I see with dogs who are mushers, their family is pretty tight. Very seldom do I see any trouble with the kids. Maybe it's the responsibility they had when they were growing up, taking care of and feeding the dogs. They had something to do.

I've commercial fished all my life for salmon. I've always loved Alaska. I've fished and hunted. I've met a lot of people, and the best people I've met anywhere are dog mushers, people who ran dogs. I hope there's always a Redington in the race. I think there will be.

RACE RECORD

1975	19 days, 7 hours, 27 minutes	17th
1977	18 days, 15 hours, 53 minutes	22nd
1988	14 days, 1 hour, 33 minutes	15th
1989	12 days, 15 hours, 22 minutes	18th
1990	13 days, 3 hours, 54 minutes	11th
1991	13 days, 13 hours, 57 minutes	10th
1992	11 days, 17 hours	15th
1993	11 days, 23 hours, 49 minutes	19th
1994	10 days, 22 hours, 39 minutes	5th
1995	9 days, 10 hours, 52 minutes	3rd
1996	9 days, 21 hours, 53 minutes	6th
1997	9 days, 21 hours, 37 minutes	7th
1998	10 days, 14 hours, 53 minutes	19th
1999	10 days, 21 hours, 15 minutes	14th
2000	9 days, 20 hours, 55 minutes	10th
2001	12 days, 8 hours, 14 minutes	26th
2002	10 days, 17 hours, 20 minutes	27th

CHAPTER 7
BILL COTTER

Bill Cotter, fifty-seven, of Nenana, came to Alaska in 1970 after graduating from Suffolk University in Boston. He jumped in a van with some buddies and drove to Fairbanks. After camping for a few days and surveying the surroundings, Cotter's friends were ready to drive back east. Cotter, who grew up in New Hampshire, felt at home and stayed.

Cotter became a teacher in Palmer in 1972 and rented a house down the street from Joe Redington Sr. Cotter began his dog-racing career that year in the Fur Rendezvous World Championship Sled Dog Race.

As his hobby became more serious, Cotter switched from teaching to summer construction work. Cotter competed in his first Iditarod in 1975 and became a full-time professional musher in 1987 after winning the one-thousand-mile Yukon Quest. He considers his victory in the Quest the dividing line in his career. His best finish in the Iditarod is third, in 1995.

Winning the Quest meant a lot because it showed that my efforts had paid off. I had worked a long time to be successful in the sport and had raised every dog team myself. So it was very meaningful to me.

It took a long time, but I'm a patient person. All of the new mushers you meet today are "McDonaldized." They want to buy a dog team and go to a store and buy all of their lines, harnesses, and snaps. They buy it all in one day and then they're a dog musher. When I started, you couldn't buy a harness. I borrowed a harness from this guy, Charley Bassett. I took it all apart and made a pattern, and we—my wife at the time, and I—sewed our own harnesses.

Today, nobody knows how to make a harness. You can buy them in a store for fifteen bucks. I made all of my own lines. It's an industry now.

Early in my first Iditarod, in 1975, I had a dream that the *Anchorage Daily News* had a headline, "Musher freezes to death in sled bag." I left the Rohn River at one in the morning, a full moon out, and very cold. I started up the south fork of the Kuskokwim River and started to get into overflow without any trail. My lead dog started to break through the ice, and when he got up another dog was breaking through. Finally the whole team went under the ice and my sled went under. The water was at least up to my knees.

I was smart enough to tie my mitts around my neck so they wouldn't get wet, and I walked up to my leader. I could feel the ice going as I walked. I sort of panicked. I really thought I was going to drown. No one else was around.

I tried to get my leader back onto the ice, but we fell down again in at least four feet of water. You never know how deep the water is. You could drop into a ten-foot hole. All of a sudden I got completely calm. My fear went away. My heart rate slowed. I just put my head up and gauged that it was a quarter of a mile to shore in either direction. But there was a little island about 150 yards up the river.

I started for the island. I would get up on the ice, break through again with the dogs floundering, trying to keep their heads above water, and go again. As I got closer, the water got shallower. The ice didn't break as much, and about twenty feet from the island I

hit shelf ice. The dogs got up into the snow, dug in, and buried themselves to get dry.

I was soaked after being in the water for about twenty minutes, and there was no firewood. I was freezing. But my mitts were dry. It was just a miracle I was able to get my hands warm. If you lose the dexterity in your hands, you're really in trouble. And I had bunny boots. I just walked around that island for four hours until it started to get light. I didn't eat. The food in my sled was frozen solid.

When it got light, I took an ax out of the sled and cut into the ice to see if it was safe. It had gotten colder. It was probably minus-fifty. The ice had frozen all over, even where I came through. I spent half an hour chopping ice off the sled. My clothes had frozen. They were hard as a rock and they were hard to walk in, but on the inside they felt like a little cave.

It was a very close call. That was the only time I thought I was going to die in the Iditarod. It was a pretty dramatic experience. I remember it clearly, like it was yesterday.

I went on and finished seventeenth in the race. But I lost thirty pounds in that race. I started it weighing 160 pounds—I'm five-foot-seven—and I weighed 130 pounds when I was done. I was out there nineteen days, not nine days like it is now. Nineteen days in the wilderness and a lot of minus-thirty, minus-fifty nights, you lose a lot of weight.

After I did my first Iditarod in 1975 and a second one in 1977, I didn't race it again until 1988. I worked construction and did sprint races and shorter races. I didn't have to put as many miles on the dogs. I have a bunch of trophies from those races. My life wasn't focused on winning the Iditarod. I was running the dogs, the kennel, working. Then they started the Quest.

When the Iditarod started in 1973, I was the first checker at the first checkpoint. Being the checker in that first Iditarod made a big impression on me. All of the guys who went were the first finishers, and they were—and still are—a big deal. When they started the Quest, I wanted to be one of the first racers. I finished third.

I went four years in the Quest, and I was involved in distance racing again. I won the Quest, and it was so cold I didn't want to run it again. It was fifty below the whole race. So I decided I was going to try the Iditarod again.

Twenty below to me is like the middle of the summer. Thirty below, there's a little temperature change where you've got to watch your hands. Forty below becomes an effort. At fifty below, it's very dangerous. You've got to keep your body moving almost all the time. On the sled I would pedal, and I never slept from Eagle to Circle. I think it took me seventy-two hours. At thirty or forty below, I can still put booties on with bare hands. At fifty below, I can't.

I had a bad experience in the '86 Quest at fifty below. I was booting a dog and he jumped up to kiss me, or whatever. His big canine on the right-hand side hit my two front teeth and snapped them off at the gum line. After that, every breath was torture. Every breath I took would burn the roots or nerves. I tried to keep my mouth closed. It was all bloody. I was about eight days into the race, and I had four days to go like that. That was one of my worst mushing experiences.

If it's fifty below when I'm home, I don't leave the house to train. If you're in a race and you're caught out in it, you just go. You get the dogs into a trot where they don't breathe that heavily in the cold and frost.

Fairbanks has a reputation for being very cold, but it is usually five or ten degrees colder at my house than it is there. Officially, the coldest it's been in the twenty-three years I've lived in Nenana was minus-sixty-five degrees. But it's been colder. It was about seventy-five below once, but it was unofficial. When I feed the dogs a stew, I mix it up inside and take out one bucket at a time. I add water to it in a five-gallon bucket. On that day, by the time I had gotten halfway through emptying the bucket, the food was so frozen I couldn't ladle it out. I would run inside, put it down, grab a new bucket, and go as far as I could.

I went back to the Iditarod, and there was a stretch between 1994 and 1997 when I finished fifth, third, sixth, and seventh. My favorite, certainly my best performance, was the 1995 race.

I remember that it was warm starting out in Anchorage, as usual. That's always a disadvantage for a team from the Interior. Anything much higher than twenty below is hard, because the dogs have developed a thick coat. That's why the first day was kind of a struggle.

Getting to Flathorn Lake, it was too hot. I forced myself to park while all of these teams were whizzing by. I watered the dogs, gave them snacks and stuff. Five o'clock came and it cooled down. I took off at a very fast run to Yentna and just went right through to Skwentna. Then I knew that these dogs were a good team. DeeDee Jonrowe, who is a good friend, and I, made a real fast run to Finger Lake.

I passed Rick Swenson on the way to Finger Lake, so I knew I had a fast team. I forced myself to stay there eight hours. It's hard to hold back. There's pressure letting Charlie Boulding hook up and go when you're parked and sitting on a cooler, waiting for time to go by. But I learned to stay at Finger Lake, and to let the dogs rest and try to get some rest for myself.

I didn't stay very long at all at Rainy Pass. I went down the Dalzell Gorge, and there was a lot of water going into Rohn. The dogs went right through the water. A lot of people got wet, but we just went flying through. It was twenty below. I was on the runners, but my feet got wet. Overflow is difficult to go through if you don't have really strong-headed leaders. You end up getting off and leading.

DeeDee's pretty competitive. She really wanted to go. She had a hard time sitting still, too, so she talked me into going. I wanted to rest more, but we left after four hours and went straight to Nikolai. We were the first two teams in. There were still ten people who could win the race, though.

Martin Buser was parked next to me, and I remember him just staring at me when I booted up my dogs after four hours' rest. I was thinking we were there first and we'd had rest and my team was really strong. All the way to McGrath, DeeDee and I kept passing each other. I was a little faster, so I came into McGrath and I got a gold watch. I was pretty happy with that. That was new to me; I hardly ever got to checkpoints first.

I declared my twenty-four-hour layover in Takotna. Martin stayed there, and Boulding and Swenson. Doug Swingley kept going. We sat around talking about how it was going to backfire, but he didn't come back to us.

It's a long run from Takotna to Iditarod (ninety miles), but it's only twenty-five miles to Ophir. DeeDee and I stopped there to throw a snack at the dogs. Martin went right by. That's when I saw how strong his team was. I was thinking, Ahh, I don't know about that team.

Hey, if you're running in the top five in the race, you've got a pretty good team. We made two jumps, cutting rest. I saw Swingley. I was checking him out. But I was getting there needing rest, and he was getting ready to leave. He looked pretty good leaving, but I cut my rest from six hours to four. I had to make a move.

I think other people who have won races will tell you that your best races, the races you finish the highest, are the easiest. Fewer things go wrong, you don't get tired, you kind of catch the wave. When you're off the wave, you struggle. I've had lots of those. When something happens and you're eight hours behind the front and it's only two hundred miles into the race, you think, Oh, crap.

It becomes difficult to keep your focus when the guy in front of you isn't in sight. In the Iditarod, that happens to almost everyone at some point. You're not racing for first, you're racing for position. If you're not in the top ten, you just want to get as high as you can. You know that if someone is eight hours ahead of you, you're not going to catch up. The race would have to be 5,000 miles, not 1,100. You're not in control anymore. Some disaster would have to happen at the front.

We were racing in good, clear weather, minus-twenty. The trail was kind of icy, though. DeeDee left Iditarod first, and I caught her later. I knew I was gaining speed on her and that her team was slowing down. When we were coming into Shageluk, a snowmachiner came out to greet us and traveled alongside. "How fast are you going?" I asked. He said he was going fifteen miles an hour.

I went into Anvik, signed in and signed out, and went on to Grayling, thinking those guys were pulling away from me. I didn't think they were gone yet, but then out of Grayling I realized I wasn't going to see Doug. I thought maybe we would see Martin again.

Doug won by a lot. He won by going on to Iditarod and not stopping at Takotna. He came off his twenty-four-hour rest one hundred miles fresher. Whatever gamble was involved in that strategy worked for him. It was so exhilarating to be up there that I didn't feel any disappointment knowing I was not able to win the race.

At Koyuk, I knew I was going to have my best finish. I was there when DeeDee came in. Martin had left maybe two hours earlier. I could see the other guys, Boulding and Jeff King and Rick Mackey, coming across the ice. I said to DeeDee, "Let's give them the empty nest syndrome." She was worried that they were going to get more rest and catch us from behind. But I said, "Let's just go. If they come in here and see you gone, they're gonna be demoralized."

Seeing Martin inspired me. I thought, Maybe he's tiring. Those guys are gonna come in and they're gonna be tired, and we're gonna be gone. They're gonna give up, or they're gonna stay there and rest. Either way, they're not gonna leave five minutes after they get here, no matter what.

At White Mountain we had the mandatory eight-hour layover. I wasn't tired; I don't think I even slept. I felt great. I went up to the lodge and took a shower. Like I said, you get on that wave.

The last stretch from Safety, I was just really grateful. I enjoyed it so much and the dogs were just motoring. Just an awesome dog team. The only sadness I had was that I knew it would never happen again with that team, with those dogs. You get close to the dogs for nine or ten days of intense, personal communication, and you know the team will never be together again. By the next year, you know there will be a half-dozen new members. So you know that closeness, that bond, is going to end.

Swingley finished in 9 days, 2 hours, 42 minutes. That was a new record. Martin was six hours behind him, and I was two hours behind Martin with 9 days, 10 hours, 52 minutes. I was a little disappointed that I didn't catch up with Martin. It would have been nice to beat him because he was a champion, but there were other champions behind me. When people say, "What's the best you ever did?" and I say, "Third," I know that's pretty good company.

It sounds odd, but I'd rather be third than second. The press, the media, all your friends, everybody—they all put tremendous pressure on you because they think you're going to win the next year, so it ruins the next year. I've seen it over and over again, where people who finish second have disastrous runs or disastrous years because it's just too much pressure.

So if I'm not going to win, I'd rather be third. I don't think many people would agree with that. In third, though, they kind of leave you alone. You get good coverage. People think you can do well. Second is expectation.

Looking back, it seems funny that I thought I was not going to do the Iditarod after the first couple of times. It obviously became very important to me. I've completed it seventeen times. I've never scratched, never been disqualified. It's a very big part of my life.

Dog mushing became a profession for me, but it's very rewarding. I've raised dogs, helped in birthing—actually taken pups from the mother and dried them off—and three years later had those pups finish the Iditarod on my team. It's been a good life, a rewarding life, and it's given me motivation to build my home and keep myself healthy. It's given me focus, and finishing well in the Iditarod is a payoff for doing what I love.

I love dogs, and if there wasn't an Iditarod I would still have a bunch of dogs. This is my way of showing off what kind of animal I have. I think I will always stay connected to the Iditarod. I don't know if I'll keep running it. At the 2002 finishers' banquet in Nome, I gave my retirement speech.

I had a lot of emotional and financial turmoil for two years, and I had my two worst finishes, twenty-fifth and twenty-sixth. I felt that I wasn't competitive anymore. I always promised myself I would quit if I wasn't competitive. When I told them in Nome I wouldn't be back, they gave me a standing ovation. Glad to get rid of me, I guess. I didn't feel like a failure because I never won the race. It doesn't really bother me at all. That's one reason I could retire.

A few months passed, and I started feeling better about everything. Rick Swenson called me and said he hated to hear me say those words. He said, "All of us are getting older, and you can unretire. You can change your mind. I changed my mind once, so don't let it bother you." I thought that was pretty nice. Maybe I'll be like Michael Jordan and retire five times.

RACE RECORD

1981	15 days 7 hours, 2 minutes	28th
1991	13 days, 14 hours, 24 minutes	12th
1992	11 days, 10 hours, 40 minutes	6th
1993	10 days, 15 hours, 38 minutes	1st
1994	10 days, 21 hours, 46 minutes	3rd
1995	9 days, 18 hours, 52 minutes	7th
1996	9 days, 5 hours, 43 minutes	1st
1997	9 days, 15 hours, 35 minutes	3rd
1998	9 days, 5 hours, 52 minutes	1st
1999	10 days, 10 hours, 10 minutes	7th
2000	9 days, 8 hours, 44 minutes	3rd
2001	10 days, 7 hours, 19 minutes	3rd
2002	9 days, 10 hours, 42 minutes	6th
2003	9 days, 23 hours, 17 minutes	3rd

CHAPTER 8
JEFF KING

Jeff King's early fascination with trapping while growing up in California led him to Alaska and to dog mushing. King, forty-eight, of Denali Park, Alaska, also grew up near Jack London State Park in the San Francisco Bay area and became familiar with the famous writer's tales of the north.

When a friend mentioned that she was interviewing for a job in Alaska, it caught King's fancy. He put up a sign on the wall of his room at Shasta College that read "Alaska or Bust." He made it to Alaska in 1975, where he obtained a summer job at Denali National Park. Later, King obtained his first dogsled ride from the National Park Service.

King, wife Donna Gates, an artist, and their three daughters operate Goose Lake Kennels. King has won innumerable middle distance races, the Yukon Quest, and three Iditarods, in 1993, 1996, and 1998.

My first race in 1977, my team was incredibly shell-shocked at the starting line. The dogs didn't bark, they didn't pull, they were just scared lying under my truck. I remember thinking, By god, I'm lucky if they go at all. But when the countdown came, they did go and they went fine.

I never dreamed my dogs could go so fast for seventeen miles. It was really, really, really fun. My next race was the Gold Miner's Classic. I made the assumption that I would really fill my dogs up because seventy-five miles, my god, I didn't know that they could even go that far. So I just fed, fed, fed them. At the starting line in Nenana, I remember Jerry Riley coming up to me and looking at my dog Boots, who was a male, and asking me if that dog was pregnant. And sure enough, Boots puked during the first ten miles of the race.

I've figured a few things out since then. But I had an absolute blast out there. I came in third place and I beat Jerry Riley. I was highly competitive in high school wrestling and football, and I hadn't done anything in the three or four years since I left college. The competitive feeling came back with a vengeance.

In 1981 I entered the Iditarod for the first time and finished twenty-eighth. I had a 104-degree fever at the end, and they put me in the infirmary with pneumonia. I don't remember much of the last third of the race. It rained going up the Anvik River—that was the only year the race went that way. And the Anvik River just completely broke up and opened up. People about drowned.

The rain was just saturating; I wore a garbage bag for a raincoat and wondered what the hell I'd gotten myself into. I withdrew in 1982. I just couldn't do it again, yet. I did a lot of other races, but I remember thinking I couldn't keep up with the Iditarod. I felt all of those guys had a jump on me. They'd been doing it for years already.

When the Yukon Quest was proposed, it was a front-page story. I thought, Now, that is the one I'm gonna do. I'm gonna be in on the ground floor. There will be nobody with more experience in this race than I, and I will put my eggs in this basket for a while. I was in every one until 1990. And I won in 1989.

In 1989 Joe Runyan won the Iditarod, and we raced in the Coldfoot Classic. I had won the Quest. I told my dad that I wanted

to win, and I wanted Joe to be second so there wouldn't be any confusion as to who had the best team. And in the end, that's exactly what happened. I came in first and Joe Runyan was second. I thought, By god, that means I'm ready to compete in the Iditarod.

In 1991 I came back to the Iditarod and finished twelfth, and the next year I was sixth. I knew that winning it was not a stretch. You have to have some things go right, just like I believe you must today. But I also thought that it was just a dog race, and that I had won all of those other races and there was no reason this one would be any different.

Boy, did I ever have to keep looking behind me the whole race. In retrospect, that made it so sweet, so much better. It was not easy for a second. Right to Safety, I was sweating.

I remember being with the front group into Shageluk, Anvik, and Grayling. I was first onto the Yukon and took a break. When I pulled into Grayling, I remember Jack Niggemyer, the race manager, on the snowbank looking at his watch. He said I had the fastest time from Anvik to Grayling.

And it was by a lot. To myself, I said, "You're kidding." In retrospect, I was the only one who had rested in Anvik, so I was bound to have the fastest time. But the big shots were in front of me, and I had a faster time. Then I found out that no one had left Grayling yet. It dawned on me that, Hey, I have something here. I decided I wasn't going out first. I had a fast team. I was going to stoke the stove. I was not going to open the draft. We were barely over halfway, so I parked the dogs and rested.

Between Grayling and Eagle Island I passed everyone. DeeDee Jonrowe was the last one, and I watched her light fade away from me. I saw how much time I was gaining on her and thought, Whoa. I was going a mile an hour faster, and I could tell I was just walking away from her. After that, we had a little cat-and-mouse thing going to Kaltag. I was with DeeDee at Old Woman cabin, leading the race, when Rick Mackey went by with twenty dogs. We were watching this team go by, and it went on and on. I said, "Holy mackerel." Just by the sheer numbers of dogs he had left, it was a little overwhelming. After Koyuk, it was an intense race between Mackey, DeeDee, and me.

We left Elim together, but it was only DeeDee and me arriving in White Mountain. Rick said, "I gotta stop. Those guys got me. If I'm going to get through it, I need to cool my jets."

DeeDee had a good run out of White Mountain, but my dogs were loping. I have some photos of them, and I can see them all stretched out. It was mostly daylight as we raced. I looked back over the hills, and there she was, man, running, pedaling, running, running, pedaling. She'd be closer, then she was farther back, then she was closer. She never seemed closer than when I got to the Topkok cabin, the shelter cabin at the bottom of the Topkok Hills. I looked back up the hill, and it seemed like she was right there. Then she came over the hill, and I thought, Oh, my god. Not just her light, I could see her. I was flying and she was right here. I was worried.

We were about fifty miles from Nome. But between there and Safety it got dark, and seeing DeeDee come down off of Topkok lit a fire under me. I did everything I could to keep the team going as fast as it possibly could. I think it worked to her disadvantage when it got dark enough for her to turn on her headlamp. She had an incredibly powerful light that made her seem so close, and that pushed me all the harder. How could she not be gaining, with the light so bright behind me?

Well, she wasn't. She was thirty minutes behind me in Safety, but I didn't know that.

I was sweating bullets at Safety. I don't remember hearing that she was thirty minutes back until I hit the beach coming into Nome, about four miles from the finish. I finally became calm when they said on the radio that she was twenty or thirty minutes back, at Safety.

I listened to the spotter car, and I heard them saying they had never seen a team coming in this fast at the end of a race. It just encouraged me. My dogs were definitely on a roll, and I had great pride in what this guy was saying on the radio.

It was pretty darned fun to approach the finish in the evening. It's so cool to see Nome when you're in the dark, to see the lights. They light up the sky a bit. But some hill blocks it. It was late enough that the kids had been put to bed, because Donna had to wake them up and get them down to the finish line. They were pretty sleepy.

It was a pretty nice scene at the finish. I waited for DeeDee to come in, and we had a big hug and a kiss. The picture was on the front page of the newspaper. I didn't have much chance to enjoy the win, though. Over the next forty-eight hours I was lambasted by animal rights activists. It went from great to horrible. Only later did I get to do some pretty neat stuff. I threw out the first pitch at a Seattle Mariners game.

Winning meant a lot, for sure. There always are, and there always will be, naysayers who think you can't do it. Some of the past champions were very vocal about who they thought might and might not be able to win the Iditarod, and I certainly wasn't on that list when I thought I ought to be. I felt I had proven myself fair and square.

Each of my wins has been special in its own way, but the most rewarding race was 1996. That was because of C. J. Kolbe. They began the Iditarider program, where fans get the chance to ride in a sled out of Anchorage at the ceremonial start. I learned before the race that I was going to have a little boy in my sled through the Make-A-Wish Foundation program, which makes wishes come true for terminally ill children. C. J. was nine years old, and he had cancer.

During the mushers' meeting two days before the race, we broke for lunch and I got to meet C. J. and his family. We had had discussions beforehand about issues for his health and the rigors of riding, and whether there would be any limitations. It was going to be only seven miles, but I took him all the way to Eagle River, so he went twenty miles.

Afterward, I remember him shuffling around the dog truck on his one leg and stump, petting all of the dogs. A lot of newspaper guys were trying to talk to C. J. and me, and I told them to stand back and let him enjoy the dogs. I don't begrudge any of them a story, but I wanted him to have a little privacy. It was neat that we supported this cause, and he enjoyed it when he was interviewed at Sullivan Arena. He was kind of digging that.

Each year, the day before the race, we have a party at the Aurora Fine Art Gallery in downtown Anchorage, which handles Donna's artwork. C. J. got my attention and, talking very privately, said he had something he wanted to give me. When he said it was his lucky penny, I just about burst into tears. I'll never forget it. He said, "It's my lucky penny and I want you to have it." Well, come on.

My mind raced through those next seconds. *What I say here is important, to both of us. I want to get it right.* I think my mind was like a computer on fast-forward. *OK, if I say no, what does that mean?* and *If I say yes, what does that mean?* I realized I couldn't say no. I thanked him and told him I would see him in the morning.

Riding to the house where I was staying, I wondered all kinds of stuff. *What if I lose the penny? If I don't win, will he think the penny's bad luck?* I fingered the penny in a pocket, making sure it didn't fall through a crack. I was not going to lose it without my head being ripped off.

As soon as I got into the house, I went to work in the garage, designing a holder in the fingertip of a glove by tying it off. People were waiting to see me, and they were saying, "What the hell is he doing?" I eventually came out and had someone tie it around my neck. All through the night I decided what I would say to C. J. I told him that the penny being lucky didn't mean I was going to win, but that it was a lucky penny for a lot of reasons. He understood that it didn't mean I was going to win, it just meant I would have good luck for my dogs. He was headed back to have his next cancer scan; he was by no means out of the woods.

Lo and behold, it was a pretty lucky penny for me. I felt more dominant over my competitors than ever before. I felt the race was mine to lose. I ran a very fast time, finishing in 9 days, 5 hours, 43 minutes, and that was almost three hours ahead of Doug Swingley.

After the race, I returned the penny to C. J. so it would stay his lucky penny. But eventually, the cancer came back and he passed away. I stay in touch with his family, and every year we mail the penny back and forth and I carry it in the Iditarod.

I won my third Iditarod in 1998, and I'm thrilled that I've become a person who is always seen as someone who can win. I feel like my family has reason to be proud of me, and that's fun. Not that you have to win the Iditarod for your family to be proud of you. But it's kind of cool for a kid to hear, "Oh, your dad won the Iditarod."

I'm definitely not as hungry as I was before I won. But I think I can win again. I think anything that I've lost in competitiveness I've gained in smarts. In 1998 I wasn't hungry, but I had the best dog team. I fully believe that if I come to the starting line with the best dog team, I will win again. I am capable of recognizing when it's the best dog team, and I know how to drive it.

It was an interesting stretch of time in the Iditarod where only three people—Martin Buser, Doug Swingley, and I—won over eleven years. It's important to me that Martin and Doug are in the race. You could say that if one of them hadn't been there, I would have won twice more, but I want the best mushers in the race. I don't want to go away thinking, Well, I won the race, but the main person you're thinking of wasn't in it. Of course, you can't win the race if you're not there. That's been my motto from way back.

It seems to me that we must be the best, and so equal to each other that no one else can come in and win. Give me the fastest dog team, and I'll win. It won't be because others psyched me out or I psyched them out. These guys can't be psyched out. I know I once said that I wouldn't be racing by the time I was fifty, but I promised my youngest daughter, Ellen, that I'd run the Iditarod until she turned eighteen. That's six more years. I found maturity. I grew up. I realized it was the best thing for me to be doing.

And I don't need to win to enjoy it. Once that realization came to me, just the mushing was fun. I am still out there to win, but I can tell when I can do it and when I can't. That's the thing that I won't know until I'm out there. It's not until you get to Skwentna or Rainy Pass that you get a feel for the magic. Is it there? The timing? The chemistry?

About the time I won for the third time, I spoke about leaving a legacy by trying to win the most Iditarods. I haven't thought about it for a while. I don't feel a longing there. I'll leave my mark on the world with my girls.

Having my daughter Cali enter the 2003 race was fun. Nerve-racking, but fun. Having a family member in the race and helping her prepare to do well was motivation.

If I ever win the Iditarod again, I don't really care how it happens. I just want to have that magic feeling going through Skwentna, knowing it's a great dog team and it's all downhill from there.

RACE RECORD

1992	11 days, 15 hours, 38 minutes	12th
1993	11 days, 12 hours	10th
1994	12 days, 7 hours, 51 minutes	24th
1996	11 days, 7 hours, 57 minutes	25th
2000	10 days, 1 hour, 23 minutes	13th
2002	10 days, 11 hours, 20 minutes	24th
2003	10 days, 22 hours, 7 minutes	17th

CHAPTER 9
BRUCE LEE

Bruce Lee, fifty, of Denali Park, has made his mark in several states and in several ways along the Iditarod trail. He grew up in Shepherdsville, Kentucky, finished high school in Michigan, earned a degree in wildlife biology from Michigan State, and became a rock climber in New Mexico, where he met someone who had just climbed Mount McKinley.

When Lee learned that it could take a month to climb the 20,320-foot peak that is the tallest in North America, he was impressed. He had always talked about going to Alaska, and this encounter prodded him to move north in 1976. After marrying his wife, Jeralyn, he moved to the Kobuk River Valley in the Brooks Range. By his second year in the state, Lee owned sled dogs, mostly for backcountry travel.

At the time, he intended to use his huskies for trips into remote areas so he could climb mountains. Ultimately, Lee realized that he enjoyed the dog team more than climbing.

Lee entered his first thousand-mile Yukon Quest in 1986 (he won the race in 1998) and his first Iditarod in 1992. He has taken years-long breaks from the Iditarod but always returns. Lee has also worked the trail as a race official and once as a field manager for the USA television network. Each summer, for three months, Lee and Jeralyn provide narrative and wildlife interpretation talks to tourists on bus rides through Denali National Park.

The 2003 Iditarod was my seventh race, but I've been out on the Iditarod Trail a lot more. My wife, Jeralyn, and I ran the course before I raced it, just to learn it.

The main reason I keep coming back to the Iditarod is the whole sport and lifestyle. We have people whose whole lives focus purely around the Iditarod. But I've run the Quest, the Rocky Mountain Stage Stop in Wyoming. I've tended to take two years and go run this kind of race and then that type of race, because I'm more interested in what dogs can do and how they were used historically.

In 1999 I had the chance to be field coordinator for USA TV, and it gave me an opportunity to be better rested on the trail. One thing that's hard for spectators and people who follow this event to realistically understand, unless they have been out there and have personally witnessed it, is how tired we are, how focused we are on our dogs, and how we sometimes say rude and obnoxious things totally with blinders on.

If you watch athletes in an Olympic event, you'll see that they're really focused. Now add a week of sleep deprivation. I think it's actually amazing how civil people can be to one another under those circumstances. Being out there filming, I had the chance to see the entire event. It's not living history. It's not a re-enactment. It's not a group of people saying, "Hey, let's get a bunch of mules and wagons and go over the Oregon Trail and see what it was like." It is a total event happening right now. The Iditarod, though it honors an historical event, is not a re-enactment.

There aren't very many things like that in the world. There are very few landscapes like Alaska where you can travel a thousand miles. It is, of course, the dogs and putting together a team that is the challenge for a musher. But it's also the whole cultural event. It's the Native communities. It's running across the frozen ice pack. It's seeing wildlife out there. It's dealing with the elements: wind and snow and cold and too much heat and too little snow. It really hit me what a unique event it is and how privileged I had been, not just to watch it but also to be in it. And I said, "I want to do this again," though sometimes it is a love-hate relationship.

In my perfect world I would much rather be respected as a good

dog person, one who breeds and
trains good race dogs and spends
tons of time with them out on
the trail, camping, traveling, and
then promoting those dogs in
other peoples' kennels who want
to race. I know mushers who, in
my opinion, care less about raising and training dogs. They want
dogs so they can race. I race to
have dogs.

I enjoy figuring out genetics
and planning breeding, but to all of us who have done this for a
long time and raced professionally, the goal is to get that one magic
carpet ride. For me, that was the Quest in 1998. I had finished fifth,
fourth, second, and third, so the only thing left was to win. It was
kind of like going to college and turning in a master's thesis. The
goal was to win or go home, and it all clicked. It would be wonderful
to have that happen in the Iditarod.

I was moving back and forth between the Western Brooks Range
and the Denali Park area, but we decided we had to have a base
on the road system. You need a place to leave a vehicle; you need
a place to live in the summer. So we bought this piece of property
and started our house. That was in 1985. Our dog team hauled
every log about three miles from the Parks Highway.

Ed Foran, who is an Iditarod finisher and who now lives in
Colorado, was a friend of mine. He had this incredible mind when
it came to the sport, just like people who are really into baseball
and can tell you how many hits some guy got and what year. He
was like that with dogs. I would go out with Ed and Jeff King and
do training runs.

They were both going to run the Yukon Quest, and we were
training in the Minto Flats by Old Minto. They said that since I had
done all of the same training runs and my team was just like their
teams, why don't I enter the Quest and travel it with them. So my
rookie thousand-mile race was the Quest in 1986. I finished twelfth
and thought, Wow, this is another challenge and a whole other way
of looking at dogs. Not just as transportation, but as athletes—just
like people do who are seriously into racing horses.

I always say that racing with a horse is easy: it's got only one head and four feet. We have to do it with sixteen or twenty dogs. We've got that many more feet to take care of, and they've got to work together. I just found it an amazing challenge. I've run the Quest five times.

Even when I was taking backcountry trips with my wife and I wasn't yet racing, we always carried a transistor radio and heard the Quest and Iditarod reports.

In 1991 I finished second in the Quest. I lost to Charlie Boulding by 4½ minutes because I didn't take him seriously. I learned a lesson there. I had already decided that the next year I was going to run the Iditarod.

I was an Iditarod rookie in 1992, and anyone who is a student of the race recognizes that some people are just in way over their heads. I didn't feel like that. I knew I could finish the race, but I didn't understand the strategies of the trail.

I decided to be a sacrificial lamb that year and run at the front of the pack until I couldn't, or until I could see things spiraling out of control. This is totally opposite from the advice I would give to a rookie now. I would say to take it easy, go slow, get familiar with the thing, and then from the halfway point, if things are going well, push.

I knew how to feed dogs. I knew how to take care of dogs in competition. I needed to learn the strategy of the trail. I ran most of the race between seventh and tenth place, and then when the team slowed down toward the Bering Sea coast, I backed off a little and placed twelfth. I also lost rookie of the year. About seventy miles from the finish line, I got passed by a gentleman named Doug Swingley, who did get rookie of the year and, of course, has won the race four times now.

One thing I learned was that I needed different types of dogs than I used in the Quest. Smaller dogs, with a different type of gait; a lighter-boned dog, because in the Iditarod you can have a bigger team and the terrain is not as steep. You look at the elevation changes on the Yukon Quest and you can tell you need some horsepower; you need some low gear. Four-wheel drive would be a good way to put it.

One reason I was interested in doing the Iditarod was that it's later in the year and there is more daylight. I think to most Alaskans the two greatest months of the year are March and, depending on which area you live, August or September. If you like being outdoors, March is just a killer. I thought, Why am I racing dogs in February when I could be racing in March? Traditionally, the Iditarod also tends to be warmer. Not that there aren't cold spells and big storms. Check the record, and you'll see that the 1992 race was one of the coldest Iditarods ever.

I don't think it ever got above minus-thirty-five; that was kind of a disappointment. Having the team slow down and not getting rookie of the year was disappointing too. What I did enjoy was going out and learning from people like Jerry Austin and Rick Swenson.

I did some things I didn't want to do. I changed my plan in Rohn; I told myself I wouldn't take my twenty-four-hour rest there. I wanted to go to McGrath or Takotna, but I was sitting in the cabin with 150 years of Iditarod experience all saying that if we went out there it would be miserable. Doug went, and he got rookie of the year. Another person blasted out and decided to gamble without trail breakers; that was Martin Buser, and that was his first win. In retrospect, I should have had more gumption and gone.

The Iditarod's a big, intimidating thing your first time, even with a lot of mushing experience. I just wanted a graceful finish. Everybody recognizes that competitors of the highest level are in the Iditarod. Your first race is kind of like climbing over the ropes with Muhammad Ali for the first time. You're going to get hit a few times.

Maybe my weakness is that I never totally made it my goal to win the Iditarod. What was important to me was just feeling competitive among teams that veterinarians and fellow competitors appreciated for being in good condition. Each individual time, it's the challenge of the event. The experience is in the people I travel with and the communities I get to go through. Basically, I'd run the whole Iditarod just to get to the Bering Sea coast. They could just fly us to the coast and I could take off. I love those coastal Eskimo villages. I hate that we spend such a short time in places like Elim. They should make it mandatory that we stay in those villages a day.

I like that country. I actually live in similar country, once you get away from Denali National Park. The Iditarod is a chance to be out and interact with the country, with people whom you sometimes get into real heavy competition with and are aggressive toward, but who under it all are almost like family. I think most people fight with their brothers and sisters while growing up, but someone on the playground who shoves your little brother had better be ready to fight the whole family.

The Iditarod is the kind of thing where there are huge rivalries, but we also have bonds.

After digesting everything I learned my rookie year, I wanted to have a better finish when I entered the Iditarod again in 1993. I wanted to be in the top ten. I wanted to be in the top ten with a chance of winning. If you aren't doing that, you might as well be going camping, having a good time, sleeping, and drinking coffee.

I went out with the leaders. I now knew places where I thought it was important to give the dogs a break. Instead of being a rookie and having to play off of other mushers, I knew where I was going. I could do my food drops more efficiently. I had set up a schedule. I had more confidence in myself, and, going back to that event in Rohn, I now felt that I didn't care if all the other guys were going or sitting. I don't care if it's a stupid thing to do, it's my privilege to make my own choice. The veterans are always psyching out insecure rookies and up-and-coming mushers. That's partially the way they defeat them.

Until you've been on that level, trying to win one of those top-ten positions, you haven't really played those kind of mind games. Someone new who wants to win has to be a real student of the race. Basically, you have to have someone coach you on an awful lot of things and have everything go right. You would just have to have an incredible team, and maybe not be taken seriously by the leaders. Races have been won that way.

I was up there in 1993, but I stopped seeing the leaders at about Ophir. Until then, I was at the front of the pack, pretty much traveling on schedule with everybody else. What I did was decide that I didn't need to be stopping for rests at all of these checkpoints. I would just grab my bags and go, because it wasn't time to stop for the dogs. I think I just had the confidence level that I was going to run my own dogs and see where things went.

Vern Halter, Joe Runyan, Sonny Lindner, and Bill Cotter dropped back a little. Those were the people I was trying to outrun. I was trying to beat Doug because he beat me the year before, and

Doug beat me again. I finished tenth, and that was the highest finish in my Iditarod career. It was satisfying because I had improved.

I was in the top ten. That means something to those of us in the Iditarod. The first couple of times you get to run up Front Street in Nome and see that burled arch and realize you made it, is something you think about. It's a pretty neat feeling after all you've gone through. It's special running through the blue-gray hills outside of Unalakleet, where you're looking out over Norton Sound. It seems like it's always sunset when I go by. Everything is every pastel color God ever imagined glowing out there, and I'm running a dog team along this cliff-hillside looking over the water.

To be in tenth place in my second Iditarod, I figured I would continue to improve from there. Then I didn't, so it's been kind of frustrating. I keep a kennel of about sixty-five dogs, and seventeen of those are puppies. That's a smaller kennel than other professional people have. Maybe it's a factor, in the same way a small-town high school basketball or football team has a harder time against a big-city high school.

What are your chances of putting together a really good basketball team in a large high school in Chicago versus one from a Central Illinois farm town? You're just going to have more good players. Part of that is finances. Part of that is how many dogs you want to have.

Look at Jeff King, Martin Buser, and Doug Swingley, who won all of the championships for eleven straight years. The biggest difference is they don't do anything else. I live a very gifted life. I live in one of those beautiful places that people pay to come to. My house is paid for. I work only three months of the year, and the rest of the year I do exactly what I want. But if I had those three months to concentrate on my sport, that would make a difference.

We don't have any kids, but I don't want my family to go through financial sacrifices. Jeralyn is totally supportive and is an equal partner in the kennel. Even though she doesn't race, she runs dogs all the time and I could never have raced without her. She deals with a lot of major aspects of the kennel. I want the time to train, but I also want to compete gracefully, without financial concerns, so that if I don't get a paycheck at the end of it, I don't have a problem.

I appreciate this event and the opportunity to participate in it. But I like traveling. I like doing other things. There's a great big world out there and a lot of neat experiences to have. They aren't better or worse than mushing dogs, just different. At some point I'll just be off on another adventure.

That's the way I look at the Iditarod. It's a great adventure. The people I feel sorry for the most are the fans, because they really don't get to be out there and see what we get to see. They get to see us leave town, they get to see the reports and the clips and wave at us as we go through. But the special thing is that day-to-day traveling, being with your dogs, lying down on the straw with them someplace, and talking to other mushers.

Sometimes, when I'm sitting on the porch and we're talking about it, I envision the Iditarod: It's three o'clock in the morning; there are eight headlamps and everybody is kneeling in the straw. Vets and mushers are putting on booties and looking at the dogs, and steam is coming up from the cookers. Maybe it's a cloudy night, or maybe it's a moonlit night; it doesn't matter. It's the middle of the night, and people are working with their dogs. That's pretty cool.

Then: Traveling down the trail with those people and stopping at two o'clock in the morning. I'm stopped, and someone else pulls over. Maybe it's Tim Osmar. Maybe it's DeeDee Jonrowe. We all go about our jobs and work like professionals, giving the dogs snacks and paying attention to each one.

Maybe I'm taking a break, sitting there on my sled and talking with other mushers about what everybody else in the race is doing. What do you think we should do? How long should we stay here? What's going on? That is the Iditarod. Those are the moments on the trail that will be my memories.

RACE RECORD

1992	Scratched	
1994	15 days, 6 hours, 39 minutes	43rd

CHAPTER 10
BOB ERNISSE

B ob Ernisse was known as the best bartender in Alaska. He served customers at Fletcher's in the Hotel Captain Cook in Anchorage for years until his death from a fast-moving cancer at age fifty-five in June 2003, several months after discussing his Iditarod memories. But another Ernisse claim to fame was the dramatic combination of his 1992 and 1994 Iditarod races.

Ernisse began mushing when he helped his cousin, Jim Welch, a sprint-dog competitor, handle his team in the late 1980s. He also played a prominent role in organizing the Serum Run re-creation each February. The eight-hundred-mile trip from Nenana to Nome was originated by legendary explorer Norman Vaughan to commemorate the 1925 event in which mushers brought life-saving diphtheria medicine to Nome to stave off an epidemic.

Vaughan, who traveled in the Antarctic with Admiral Richard Byrd, and whose late-in-life adventures captivated Alaskans, encouraged Ernisse to enter the Iditarod, promising a unique experience. Ernisse did have a memorable Iditarod experience, but not the one he anticipated.

Isaw my first Iditarod in 1976, and I thought it was so amazing that these men and women were so adventurous. These guys would walk down the street, and everyone was watching them and saying, "Wow, this guy has been across Alaska by dogsled." Norman Vaughan told me that if I ever ran it, I'd never, ever regret it. Norman was right.

It was in the 1980s when I started helping my cousin Jim Welch train his dogs. I'd take six-dog teams or eight-dog teams out in Eagle River. In 1989 a race was coming up in Chugiak, and Jim asked me if I wanted to run it. I said, "Absolutely." Bob Hickel, my friend and boss at the hotel, ran it too. We had a great time. At the end of the day, Bob looked at me and said, "You know, if we can do this, we can do the Iditarod." Both of us laughed. The difference is only 1,100 miles.

Bob signed up to run his first Iditarod in 1990. He leased a team from Dewey Halverson, who came in second in the 1985 Iditarod behind Libby Riddles. We were helping Bob train the dogs, and one day Dewey turned to me and said, "You know, Bob, you ought to run the Iditarod." I said, "I've been thinking about it." Dewey bet me five dollars that I would never, ever do the Iditarod.

In 1992 I signed up to run the race. I spent a little over $40,000 to train and lease a team. By the way, Dewey Halverson has never, ever given me that five dollars. For a while Dewey had a dog exhibit about the Iditarod at Denali National Park. Tourists would come into town and stop at Fletcher's, and tell me that they were going to the park. I told them they needed to see Dewey's dog-and-pony show, and that when he was all done and asked for questions, to raise their hands and ask, "Are you ever going to give Bob Ernisse that five dollars?"

I leased a dog team from Laird Barron in the fall of 1991. I ran the Klondike 200 and came in eighth. Had a great time. I was a rookie musher at age forty-three.

It was just as hard a job to get sponsors, but the Captain Cook was behind me and the community was behind me. I've been voted the best bartender five times now through the *Anchorage Daily News*. My reputation helped me—amen, brother—but I think the

community came behind me because I was a wannabe musher.

Laird warned me that I was going to be so nervous I would be sick to my stomach at the starting line. The main thing I was nervous about was going through Anchorage. I knew I could drive dogs without falling off the sled, but I worried that something was going to happen, that I'd have a bad tangle on Fourth Avenue in front of all those people. The dogs I had trained were not used to running in front of a crowd. Once we hit Mulcahy Park and started getting onto the back trails, I was fine.

I wanted to have an official finisher's patch. I wanted to have an official finisher's belt buckle because it's such an elite group. That was my whole goal. Go out, run the race, be with my dogs, see the country of Alaska, and have fun. I did. Even though it was the coldest race in the history of the Iditarod. It was minus-fifty in McGrath. It was the only time in my life the enamel of my teeth hurt. And I had a full face-mask on. I had all of my mushing gear on, a beaver hat, face mask underneath the hat, and another scarf over the face mask. It was just bone-shivering cold.

I left Knik and was headed to Skwentna, going through the alders, and all of a sudden I saw a headlight coming toward me. I thought, What the heck is this? Am I going the wrong way, or what? I stopped my dog team. The other musher came up and got into a big tangle with my dogs, and I said, "Hey, buddy, the race is the other way." It was Bob Hickel. It was the first time I saw him on the racecourse. He had stopped his dogs to rest at Flathorn Lake, then took off and left his snowshoes there, so he turned around to go back and get them.

We hooked up again at Skwentna, and he and I and Bill Bass started running together. We weren't really racing; we were all out there for the same thing, to get to Nome. Bob was already an official finisher, but Bill and I just wanted to get our patches. Mellen Shea and Debbie Corral were with us too.

At Finger Lake, Bob and Bill and I pulled in together and parked on the side of the hill. I put the snow hook in and tied my leaders off. Bill did the same thing. I asked Bob, "Aren't you going to tie your leaders off?" He said, "Nah, my dogs are pros. They've been on the trail before." He was insinuating that they weren't going anywhere. But Bob forgot one thing: his two wheel dogs were in season and his leaders were males.

So, as Bob was cooking his meal for the dogs, the leaders turned the entire team around and all sixteen of them tangled up in a circle. I said, "Hey, Bob, you know your professional leaders? Well, they're back there talking to your wheel dogs right now." It took almost forty-five minutes to get the dogs separated because they were having fun, and we had to wait until they quit having fun a couple of times. Before we finished, an airplane landed and a photographer from *The Anchorage Times* got out and said, "What do you call this?" And I said, "Professionals."

All the way down the trail, different people from the bars in Anchorage sent us musher telegrams saying they were behind us and everything else. The three of us felt like we were winning the race. At times we realized we were four days behind the leaders, but we were not out to set any records. The Iditarod was probably one of the best experiences I've ever had except for the birth of my children.

At White Mountain we took our mandatory eight-hour layover. We had a couple of cheeseburgers, fries, Diet Pepsis. We were all real excited that we had only seventy-seven miles to go. It had been uneventful along the trail; except for the cold weather, we all had good gear and we were happy. Only seventy-seven miles to go. I did it. Bill did it. Bob did it.

It had been just like Norman said, a marvelous adventure. Seeing the backcountry, coming across the Farewell Burn, seeing the bison, seeing wolves. It was wonderful. The country is absolutely beautiful. It really, really makes you believe there is a creator, that there is somebody up above who said, "Hey, I'm gonna lay this out for you guys and you ladies." It's just absolutely the most gorgeous country I've ever seen in my life.

We left White Mountain at about 11 PM. When we went over the Topkok Hills the wind was blowing. My dogs looked great; they were just stringing out super. We hit the Topkok shelter cabin about forty miles out of Nome. There was a gentleman in there with another musher and they said hello, and the guy said to be careful, there was a groundstorm.

Bill had gone ahead with Mellen Shea, and I was traveling with Bob and Debbie. We stopped at Tommy Johnson's cabin, which is about thirty-three miles from the finish line and about eleven miles from Safety, the last checkpoint. We talked and said, well, it wasn't too bad. We could see the end of our dog teams. I could see Bob in front of my team; Debbie could see me.

The wind was blowing, the snow was swirling, and it was night, but we decided we could go on, that we could get through the wind and that we had seen the worst of the storm.

We left Tommy Johnson's right at 2 AM. All three of us looked at our watches. We decided if it got bad we'd turn around and come back. Ten minutes after two, we lost the trail. The winds picked up to fifty, sixty miles an hour. We were in complete whiteout conditions. We found a trail marker blown over. The trail was completely blown out. Three big trees with reflectors on them were lying in the middle of the trail. We stopped and looked for the trail, but we couldn't find it.

We tied a gang line to Bob's waist, and he walked out in a circle to see if he could find the trail. I held the line, and when it got tight, I pulled him back so he wouldn't get lost. We looked for hours. And then we couldn't find our way back to Tommy Johnson's cabin. We were only ten minutes out!

When we turned back, my two leaders got in a bad tangle. I made a big rookie mistake. Instead of cutting the line and freeing the leaders of the tangle, I put my beaver mittens and gloves around my neck to unhook the neck lines. Within thirty seconds my hands were the color of white paper, and when I hit them together they sounded like two stones hitting each other. I put my gloves back on and we kept searching for the cabin. It was about five-thirty in the morning, but not light out yet. No sign of the cabin, and the cabin even had a strobe on top.

I told Bob, "I can't go on." I couldn't see out of my left eye because the snow was so bad, and my hands hurt so terribly that they were numb. I couldn't hold onto the driving bow of the sled. So we decided we were going to wait the storm out. Bob helped me get all of my gear out of the sled so I could climb inside. I had done some running behind the dogs at Topkok, and I had built up a pretty good sweat. And now I'd stopped moving. My core temperature was dropping rapidly.

I got inside the sled and inside my sleeping bag. But the zipper on the sleeping bag was broken. Bob tried to help me, and finally I said I would just hug it to my body and zip up the sled bag. I went to zip up the sled bag, and the zipper was solid ice, just frozen solid. There was a Velcro strip, and I pushed from inside the sled bag and Bob pulled from outside and we finally got it closed. Bob said he was going over to his sled to do the same thing if I was OK, and I said I was fine.

My coat and boots were off, though I was still wearing the boot liners, and inside the sleeping bag I kept moving my hands from my crotch to underneath my arms, back to my crotch, trying to warm them up. When they started to hurt, I realized I was warming them up a little bit and I fell asleep.

The wind kept howling and the snow kept blowing. I woke up around seven-thirty or eight in the morning, and I had two inches of snow on me. Snow had been blowing into the sled bag. I was just covered. I pushed the snow away and sat up, and the sled bag came open. I tried to stand to get my parka and I couldn't; my legs wouldn't work. So I called for Bob.

He could not hear me over the wind. He was probably twenty feet away, parked parallel to me. I kept callling, "Bob! Bob!" All of a sudden—it seemed like an hour and a half later, and me getting hoarse—it seemed as if the wind died for a minute. I heard, "What?" I said, "Bob, I'm in trouble. Come over here and help me."

Bob got his parka on and instead went over to Debbie Corral. He unzipped her sled bag and she looked at him and said, "What?" He said, "Are you all right?" She said, "Yeah, I'm fine." When Bob got to me, my sled bag was open and I was sitting there in my long johns. Ice was coming out of my nose and my face was covered with ice. He said, "You're in trouble." I said, "Bob, I can't stand up."

He lifted me up, and when he let go of me, I fell. I had to get my parka back on. Bob helped me up again and leaned me against the handlebars. He helped me put on my bib pants. He put them on backward; I had to step out of them so he could put them on again. Then I got my parka on and he put a hat on me, and all of a sudden he started hitting me. He was slapping me in the face. I looked at him and said, "Quit hitting me. If you hit me again I'm gonna hit you back. I'm gonna hurt you." Bob said, "Get mad. Get real mad. That's what you need to do."

What I found out later was that Bob hit me thirty or thirty-five times, and I only acknowledged it twice. I was in a serious hypothermic stage. I was falling asleep, and he was trying to revive me. The last stage of hypothermia is that you get hot and take off your clothes, and then you fall asleep. That's the stage I was in. If it hadn't been for Bob Hickel, I wouldn't be alive today.

Bob was saying, "Stay mad. Stay mad." We still had no idea where we were. Then we heard a voice. Bob said, "No, we need help. My partner here is in really bad shape." It was the guy from the shelter cabin. His name was Robin Taylor. He was from Nome, and he was running a mail route back and forth from White Mountain. He said he would take me on his sled and that his dogs were used to being out in these storms.

When we were about four miles from Safety, he picked up Nome radio and asked if I wanted to listen to his Walkman. I was about 90 percent conscious by then. We started listening to this interview where someone was talking about an Iditarod musher who was frostbitten and hypothermic and they were bringing him into Nome. I thought, Oh man, I hope that guy's all right.

And it was me. We got into Safety, and the paramedics had come out from Nome. Turns out the Iditarod had sent snowmachiners to find us because we were taking so long from White Mountain. But they couldn't get all the way out to where we were because of the storm.

Mike Owens, who had run the Iditarod a couple of times, was the paramedic. My main concern was my dogs; they're the heart of the race. I wanted to go back out and finish. I didn't think I was in such bad shape. I knew I was cold, but I had warmed up. I had a couple of glasses of hot Tang and was feeling a lot better. I told Mike that I wanted to go get my dogs and bring them across the finish line. He said, "Nah, you're done."

I looked at him and said, "I can do this race. I can finish this race." And he said, "Bob, if you go back out there, you're gonna lose some fingers." I asked him, "How many?" I actually had no memory of this at the time. He told me later.

Al Marple showed up—he was the race marshal—and he said, "Bob, I want you to scratch right here." I said, "No, Al. I can go back out there, get my team, and cross the finish line. We trained. The dogs ran over a thousand miles. They deserve to finish, and I want them to finish." Al said, "Nope, you're done."

Finally, he said, "How are you going to hold onto the handlebars?" I told him I would wrap a tug line around my arm and tie myself to the sled. Then he asked how I would be able to untangle the dogs. He held up a snap and ordered me to undo it. I couldn't work the snap. It brought tears to my eyes. I was really heartbroken.

They took me into Nome by pickup truck. Mike Owens got a bunch of mushers and snowmachiners together, and they went out and put my dogs into kennels and brought them into Nome.

I spent twenty-four hours in the hospital. I was hypothermic and I had frostbite on my fingers, on my face, the bridge of my nose, and my left eye. Mike came in and told me they took the dogs under the arch, and that made me feel a little better, but not much. It was a very depressing night for me. I was only thirty-two miles from the finish line. They've never had a musher scratch that close.

They had the first official finishers' banquet the night I was in the hospital, but I went to the second one, for the mushers who came in later. I was bandaged from fingertips to elbows, and I had all kinds of black around my face.

A lot of mushers came by to say hello, and several of them tried to give me their official finisher's patch, saying that I earned it. I said, "No, I didn't. I can't take it." I really wanted to, but I couldn't. John Barron insisted that I take his. He said, "I want you to go home and sew this on your coat. You deserve it as much as any musher who's here." I said no, but he left it. I took that patch home, put it on my mantel, and looked at it every day for two years.

People were heartwarming in Nome. They were all telling me what a great job I did, saying they were sorry I couldn't finish. I was in Iditarod headquarters. Montana musher Terry Adkins walked in, and he looked at me and said, "Boy, you look like you got the hell kicked out of you." I said, "I did, Terry, I really, really did." He said, "Is there anything you want?" I said, "The only thing I want is a chew of Copenhagen." Terry grinned. He chewed Copenhagen. He reached into his pocket, pulled out a big, old, two-finger chew, reached up, pulled my lip out and put it in because I couldn't use my fingers. That's a true buddy. I've quit, but since then every time I see Terry Adkins he always kids me, saying, "Hey, Bob, you want a chew?"

At the banquet the only people who get to speak are the finishers, but they called me up anyway. That was a big inspiration for me. I thanked Bob Hickel immensely—they gave him the sportsmanship award for helping me—and Mike Owens and Al Marple and everybody else. They basically saved my life. And I said, "I got real close, but it's not over with. I'm gonna come back."

When I got back to Anchorage and saw the doctor, the first thing he said was, "Did you just get off Mount McKinley?" He called in his mentor, Dr. William Mills, the frostbite expert, to look at me.

Dr. Mills told me to hold out my hand and turn around. I did, and he ran a pinwheel over my hand to judge how much feeling I had. He said, "What do you think?" I said, "Go ahead and run it." He said, "I already did."

I went to physical therapy every day, twice a day, for a month or so. I also called a friend of mine, Eddie Bodfish in Barrow, knowing he is from a very cold place and his whole family had dealt with the cold for generations, and asked what they did for frostbite. He recommended beluga whale oil and sent me some.

I went to physical therapy in the morning, and at night I rubbed whale oil on my hands. All of a sudden, I started getting the color back in my hands. I was cracking my skin off, just pulling it off, and it was starting to get pinkish. The dark blues and blackness were going away. I saw Dr. Mills and he said, "See? The physical therapy is working," and I said, "The whale oil, too. He said, "That's just a fallacy." I said, "My mind is telling me that it is working really, really well."

Every day I stared at that finisher's patch, and in 1994 I signed up to run the Iditarod again. Laird Barron and I had become partners. I raised the money for the kennel and he trained the dogs. Frostbite is always with you. Dr. Mills told me I shouldn't do the Iditarod again, but I grinned and said, "It's like climbing Mount

McKinley and having your fingers on the summit and being just about at the top and the wind blows you off. You have to go down a couple of hundred feet, but you can go back up there. It's just follow your dreams, you know, follow your dreams."

I had a great start and a great race all over again. Same bit. I traveled a lot with Steve Adkins and Ron Aldrich. Ron said, "You're gonna get there. Don't worry." The weather was great. I did wear two pairs of gloves under my beaver mittens, and I kept heat packs inside my gloves. But it wasn't cold—until we got to Topkok. I didn't leave White Mountain until daybreak that time. I wasn't going through in the dark. Coming through Topkok, the wind started blowing a little bit and I was thinking, "God, here we go again." But I got through it.

Steve Adkins got into Safety ahead of me and met my family. My lady, Sue, two of my three children, and Bob Hickel were waiting for me. They asked, "Have you seen Bob?"

They didn't recognize me when I first came in because I had on an orange windsuit and nobody knew I had it. When I pulled into Safety, Sue came up to me and said, "Have you seen Bob?"

I looked at her and said, "Hi, honey. Sure nice to smell Giorgio instead of dog." We laughed and hugged, and my kids and I hugged. Bob and I hugged. I was there for about ten minutes.

It was clear, and the wind started to die down. It was still light when I came down Front Street, about five o'clock in the afternoon. I remember seeing all of my friends at the finish line. I picked up my youngest, my son Bobby, as I came down the street. I had told him in Anchorage, "I'll see you at the beginning of the finish chute." He was staring at me and his chest was out: "My dad's here." I just scooped him up and put him on the runners. It was very cool.

I finished in forty-third place in 15 days, 6 hours, and 39 minutes. It wasn't a huge crowd waiting for me, but in my eyes all the right people were there. It was a high seeing the arch and going underneath the arch, and my family was there and they were all proud of me, and I was proud of my dogs and proud that I had gone back and done what I said I was gonna do.

I made it to the banquet about twenty minutes before it started. Dick Mackey, the former champion, presented me with my belt buckle and said I was the only musher in Iditarod history to travel more than 2,100 miles to get one.

After the banquet, a gentleman came up to me and offered me $5,000 for my belt buckle. I just looked at him and started laughing. It was very, very strange. He could have given me $100,000 and I wouldn't have sold that belt buckle. It is one of my prized possessions.

RACE RECORD

1989	13 days, 13 hours, 37 minutes	26th
1990	12 days, 1 hour, 19 minutes	8th
1991	15 days, 23 hours, 45 minutes	25th
1992	12 days, 21 hours, 59 minutes	25th
1993	11 days, 21 hours, 2 minutes	17th
1994	11 days, 15 hours, 57 minutes	18th
1995	10 days, 8 hours, 27 minutes	13th
1996	10 days, 7 hours, 25 minutes	17th
1997	10 days, 14 hours, 58 minutes	17th
1998	9 days, 22 hours, 29 minutes	8th
1999	10 days, 18 hours, 30 minutes	13th
2000	10 days, 4 hours, 1 minute	19th
2001	10 days, 3 hours, 58 minutes	2nd
2002	Scratched	
2003	10 days, 7 hours, 2 minutes	6th

CHAPTER 11
LINWOOD FIEDLER

Linwood Fiedler, fifty, lives in a log home in Willow, Alaska, with his wife, Kathi, and three children. As a youngster, he cavorted in the White Mountains of New England, where he hunted, fished, built tree houses, and yearned to emulate Ethan Allen. Fiedler developed an appreciation for the outdoors, moved to Montana in his twenties, and took up mushing. In 1990, with the goal of becoming a more serious Iditarod competitor, he moved to Alaska.

Fiedler always had an interest in dogs, and he raised German shepherds with his mother. Taking up competitive mushing combined his interests in the outdoors and dogs. He calls it a good marriage, though he describes his early mushing days as a comedy of errors and accidents.

Fiedler entered his first Iditarod in 1989, placing twenty-sixth, but progressed to second in 2001. Fiedler keeps trophies from his top-twenty finishes on display; the walls of his home also feature a large king salmon mount and a bearskin rug.

Mushing was totally for entertainment at first. I went to some racing kennels and looked at Alaskan huskies. I went to some other kennels and looked at Siberian huskies and Alaskan malamutes. I thought that if I was going to be feeding all of these dogs, I wanted a real pretty team. So I picked Siberians and Alaskan malamutes at first, and mushed them for four or five years. I entered my first race and got passed by all of the Alaskan teams. I didn't know dogs could travel that fast.

I did the John Beargrease in Minnesota and the Iditarod a couple of times while we were still living in Montana. We had always talked about moving to Alaska. Kathi was flying the trail, and she was offered a pretty high-paying job by our standards. I came into McGrath and she said, "I've been offered this great job. It's half time, and it pays more than I'm making working full-time in Montana." We went back to Montana, put our tiny ranch up for sale, and moved to Alaska.

I had finished eighth, but I discovered that racing the Iditarod wasn't always going to be so easy. In 1991, my first race living in Alaska, I placed twenty-fifth. It took a long time (1998) to get back to eighth. By 2001 I had run twelve Iditarods.

As with any athlete, my track record started defining me. I had been in the top ten or the teens a lot. But I didn't want to be someone who comes in twelfth anymore. I needed to say, "OK, that's my lot in life, about a twelfth place musher," or I needed to be better. I felt like I needed to take more risks and be willing to fail, to really put myself out there and to fail in front of everybody. I had always carried enough reserve in my team so that I could finish strong.

In 2001 I told myself, "Let's see what you can do." If I failed, the worst thing was that I would go home and lick my wounds and try again. It was a wonderful race. It snowballed, and we got happier and happier.

In training, I did a lot of camping with the dogs and stayed away from all other races. That was a change; I had been running 300s. About February I started fine-tuning our efforts.

The team was a very honest team. Because of the amount of camping I did with the dogs, I really felt that I knew their limitations

and was very tuned into that group of dogs.
We went out for a week or two at a time
with tents. We'd take the truck and pack
up and do long trips, then we'd come back
to the truck, refill supplies, and take off
again. We went to different places almost
every week.

We went out around Trapper Creek,
the base of Denali—which, of course, is
gorgeous—Cantwell, Paxson, up into the
mountains around Fairbanks. I think it
helped me build more of a bond with the
dogs. You can physically train a dog or an
athlete and get to one plateau. Then, I think what happens next is
mental training. Mushing is mental bonding between the driver
and the dogs and getting those two, the canine head and the human
head, to kind of work together.

It gets to the point where you can run seventy or eighty miles,
and the dogs come in and they're not winded. They're frisky. What
more can you do but the mental training? I think it is really key.
That certainly came together for me in 2001.

At the start of the race, I felt I had the best of all worlds; I
had a good dog team and I was going to pull out all the stops. I
also felt I was going to do it without being watched by the media
as far as being a top contender. I thought that about the top-ten
competition too. I didn't think they were really going to watch me
that carefully, because I hadn't been running in that group. It helped
me the first half of the race.

I was surprised that others didn't go out as quickly as I did. The
official start was from Willow that year. It was a warm day: no hat,
no gloves, maybe in the forties. Almost everybody ran to Yentna
and then put in a major rest of six to eight hours. But Yentna is only
forty miles from Willow, so it just didn't make any sense to me.

My plan was to run to Finger Lake and put in a major break,
then to Rohn and put in another major break. I was trying to
maximize my runs, going back to what Joe Runyan said when he
won in 1989: long runs, long rests. I was pretty much looking at
eight-hour runs with no significant stops. Maybe little stops that
lasted three and a half minutes to snack every dog, then jump back

on the sled and go. I'm talking about being able to do an eight-hour run without wiping out the team.

I had a little-black-book plan all written out. I get so tired I can't even count; I really have to count with my fingers. Over the years, I had been less plan-oriented. I've learned that I need to be the opposite. Different people run dogs differently, with equal results.

I've always been a touchy-feely sort of person with my animals. Some people who run dogs weigh them once a week and calculate this and that sort of thing. I don't. I touch them, run my hands down their backs. That's how I learn if they are overweight or underweight.

I ran mostly by gut instinct. But I learned that, as with everything in life, your strengths are often your weaknesses. So I tried to incorporate more structure, become more plan-oriented, while still keeping that touchy-feely thing because that's part of me. It was not the first time I'd tried it, but it was the first time I'd worked up a plan that I knew the animals could do, and I knew that if we stuck with the plan I'd get into the top ten. I never thought about coming in first or second; I just knew it would propel us into the front bunch. After that, I thought it was a matter of seeing how the cards fell.

Even though I had done the Iditarod twelve other times, it still intimidated me. In the past I had pushed the dogs too far, and I hated myself for doing it. I hated the results and said I would never do it again. I had been to the Bering Sea coast in terrible groundstorms where I couldn't even see my lead dog. The other thing was being afraid on the inside—a mental thing for an athlete—of being up front in the Iditarod. I had always been very good at three-hundred-mile races. I'd been up front and been comfortable. I had been able to win them or come in second against very good competition.

I decided I was going to push this Iditarod as if it were a three-hundred-mile race. I told myself it was four 300-mile races and I could feel comfortable up front. I did a lot of work on my mental outlook. I remember laughing at myself and thinking, "I feel OK being up front." I found that this race helped me learn a lot about myself. Every Iditarod, really. I think I've been able to grow and be a better man because of racing the Iditarod. The race, the trail, tests you. This race was a growing point for me, to feel comfortable and not intimidated.

I had run the race so many times that I had friends along the trail. Even the race marshals I have to obey are still my friends. Many of the people who take care of the checkpoints are the same ones who have been there for ten years. When they saw me rolling up in the lead, they couldn't help being happy. There were a lot of pats on the back, people saying, "You're doing great."

It gives you tremendous energy; you can't help but feed off it. It was one of those times where many things were in the zone, and, boy, I was loving it after finishing nineteenth the year before.

People knew me because I had run the Iditarod many times, and there was a sort of sense that the underdog was rising up and coming to the front. Even today, so much later, I will go into the grocery store and people will comment on the effort. We took chances. We tried our hardest. And it paid off. People liked that effort.

A couple of teams were there when I left Skwentna, but then I was cutting my own trail. I was in the lead for about four hundred miles. I never really felt confident, though. I knew I was winning, but my definition of winning was being in the top ten. I knew I was in a very good place for that, and I was pretty excited. I had committed to taking our twenty-four-hour layover in Anvik, the official halfway point. I didn't know what was happening behind me.

Coming into Anvik is one of the neatest experiences I will ever have on a dog team. There's an old video of a 1980s Iditarod race where Dewey Halverson and Jerry Austin took off like rabbits, and they came into Anvik leading. In the video, they're coming over the hill and the church bells are ringing. I've always thought, Gee, wouldn't that be so awesome to have that happen? And when it happened for me, it was unbelievable. I came into Anvik with tears in my eyes.

Approaching Anvik, it's pretty flat. It's just you and your dog team. The dogs were a little tired. We were doing a one-hundred-mile stretch non-stop, and they still hadn't had their twenty-four. After you wind through some swampy stuff, you break out onto the Yukon River, cross it, and come to the little village of Anvik. I could see the church and the town.

No bell was ringing, and I thought, Oh, maybe they just did this in the '80s and they don't do it anymore. I guess the mayor was scrambling up the stairs, but when I came up the hill, the bell started ringing, a steady "dong, dong." It was a meaningful, spiritual thing for me. The whole town seemed to come out, but even more people showed up when they realized I was going to stay for twenty-four hours and eat the halfway prize meal in front of them. It hadn't happened for a while; the leaders had been in too much of a hurry.

It was important to that village to have someone stay and appreciate the meal and appreciate them. It was a real big party. There were about seven courses to the meal and a bottle of wine with each one. I just had a little taste of each. The culmination of the meal was a lobster tail, the biggest I had ever seen.

Everyone was watching me eat. I asked how many people had never had lobster before, and all of these hands went up. I cut the lobster into little pieces, and the villagers came around in a line and took some. It was fun to share it. It felt good to bring some of the fun back to the race, not to be all so serious.

Doug Swingley came in with his team, and I think he took an eight-hour rest. I watched him leave in the lead. That's when I thought, I can beat this guy. He was the defending champion and had set the race record the year before, but he did not leave that impressively.

After my twenty-four-hour layover, I ran to Grayling. Sitting up on the bluff, I watched Doug leave, but his dog team did not want to leave. Jeff King was coming on. I thought Jeff might beat me, but I thought we were both going to beat Doug. I figured it was going to be between Jeff and me for first. I'll tell you, Doug had to coax that team. I don't know what he's got, but he got that team going. Next thing I knew, they were flying down the Yukon River. He made better time than I did.

Everybody who saw him leave was floored that he could get that team moving that way. I was very impressed with Doug. I was thinking, Holy cow, what happened?

Doug got a jump on me, and he was able to make better time. The Yukon River was covered with very soft snow. I think the weakness in my team was training on trails that were hard and fast. When the dogs got into soft snow, they wallowed around. They just couldn't drive through it. So I let them set their own pace and got off their cases. I just assumed it would get better later and that we would catch up.

I would come into a checkpoint and Doug would leave. I don't know if he put new leaders up there or if he'd trained his dogs to jump off the trail and look terrible. Anyway, he didn't falter again.

He got pretty much a whole rest ahead of me. Then my game plan was not to catch Doug, but to put my attention on Jeff and see how we were going to finish.

I got into Nome about eight hours behind Doug and about 3½ hours in front of Jeff. The feeling equaled how I felt in Anvik. It was a very spiritual, very joyous time. Friends and family had flown in and were excited for me and for the dogs. The community of Nome was very excited for us. There were thousands of people, all the way down the street. We were all crying, and it was just really neat and so exciting.

My wife had always told me that I could win the Iditarod. She's been more confident than I have been. It was one of the first times that I thought, Maybe Kathi's right. I can win this thing someday.

I really enjoyed the whole race. To some people winning is extremely important, but it's not that important to me. I have been able to be competitive, very competitive, in three-hundred-mile races and still have fun and still be a nice guy and be myself. I don't see why I can't do that in the Iditarod too.

I think what happens is that the front-runner gets very focused. And I think Americans expect athletes who are very good to isolate themselves from the rest of the world for eleven months to train. Then they expect them to have public relations skills and be adept in times of stress. Those are critical moments in terms of public image.

We do have, whether we like it or not, an impact. The sport has a tremendous following. If mushers want to get involved with the Iditarod, they have to realize that their behavior—what they do and say between checkpoints and at checkpoints, and before and after the race—is being watched.

I think there are a lot of good role models in the Iditarod, people who are honest with themselves and with the public. The bottom line is that even if you have won multiple times, you're still not making a huge income. You're really doing it because you enjoy the dogs, Alaska, its country, and the people along the way. You've got to have a tremendous love for this. It's too tough, too much of a sacrifice.

The 2001 race will be the one I'll always remember. If I ever win, I don't know if that will be more important to me. That race was a real milestone. It did a lot of things for me, and it will always be one of those huge races, ten days that I will remember out of my life.

RACE RECORD

2001	12 days, 17 hours, 53 minutes	33rd
2002	10 days, 18 hours, 1 minute	29th
2003	10 days, 17 hours, 17 minutes	14th

CHAPTER 12
ALIY ZIRKLE

Before settling into an existence revolving around snow, Aliy Zirkle, thirty-four, of Two Rivers, Alaska, resided in places that revolved around sand and in places that revolved around tall buildings.

The three-time Iditarod racer and the first woman to win the Yukon Quest, in 2000, spent her youth in the Caribbean (with many animals, including dogs), went to high school in St. Louis, and worked on a degree in biology from the University of Pennsylvania. After two years of college, she saw an ad for a summer job in Alaska.

Zirkle went north, sharing a wall tent with three other people for six months near King Salmon on the Alaska Peninsula, while working as a volunteer for the U.S. Fish and Wildlife Service. Later, she worked on bird studies in Australia.

After graduation, Zirkle was rewarded with a U.S. Fish and Wildlife biotech position in frigid and tiny Bettles, population thirty-five, at the foot of the Brooks Range. During her first winter, Zirkle obtained her first husky, a dog named Skunk, and her kennel is now called SP Kennels, for Skunk's Place.

When I started mushing in Bettles I got six dogs. I got most of them from people in the Athabascan villages of Allakaket, Hughes, and Huslia along the Koyukuk River, basically former world champion George Attla's stomping grounds. I always made it public that the dogs I got there were a significant part of my team. They are very proud of the dogs from that area, and they should be. I'm proud to have a lot from Koyukuk River bloodlines.

By 1996, when I came to Two Rivers, I had a great friend and mushing ally, Jerry Louden, who became my partner, and he put the little racing bug into me. I had run the Christmas race in Allakaket that was probably twelve miles. I finished third and won $800. I thought, Holy cow, you can make money at this?

I trucked my dogs forty-five miles to Allakaket. For a couple of years all of the guys knew Aliy was "up there" with some dogs—I just came down to buy one every now and then. My dogs had a couple of thousand miles on them, but they ran trapline speed and I had a big sled.

My dogs sat down at the starting line. I whistled and said, "Good dogs, good dogs." We left the line at two-minute intervals, and two minutes and fifteen seconds later somebody flew right by me. It didn't go real well, but I won a lot of money.

Then I did the Two Rivers 200 and started working toward the Yukon Quest because it was a natural progression. Plus, it starts or finishes right here in Fairbanks. I entered the Quest in 1998, and it was anyone's typical first year. You can't believe dogs can possibly eat as much as they do. You can't believe they can run as far as they do without taking a break. You can't believe you're so tired.

I bred some dogs with Jerry's, and we had a couple of nice breedings in there. In dog mushing, you're lucky to come across a fabulous dog. If you happen to breed her at the right time to another fabulous dog, four years later it's, "Holy cow, how did that happen?" The products of those breedings were dogs that were totally at their peak in 1999 and 2000. I studied everything. I had a map plastered to the wall. I was really ready to win the Quest in 2000.

The first Quest was a total education in racing: how it can be done, what you have to do to keep your dogs going, what you have

to do to keep yourself going. In 1999 I finished fourth. I was in the front pack. I learned how these guys—John Schandelmeier, Mark May, Ramy Brooks—were doing it. I'm not the type of person who would pick up the phone and say, "Hey, how do you pack food for the dogs?" or "Hey, how many booties are you taking out on the trail?" I've always learned the hard way being out on the trail. I'm hardheaded.

In 2000 I knew how great my dogs were. There were some good teams in there: Peter Buteri, Frank Turner—a past Quest champion. It helped a lot that for a centennial celebration the race was going from Fairbanks to Whitehorse the second year in a row, instead of switching to the opposite direction.

When I won, it was huge. It was actually bigger than I thought it would be. When it first happened, I thought, Well, that was great. I really wanted to win and that was fabulous. And then it blossomed and I got all kinds of attention. I talked to Libby Riddles about how she handled it when she became the first woman to win the Iditarod in 1985. We were in Maine together for a talk and compared notes.

She's made a living off of her win. A Yukon Quest win is different from an Iditarod win, but it is the second most important race in the world. It's a huge honor. It was really only a few years between my basically running six dogs and tromping around the overflow to get to the other side of the river to the finish line, to the media craze of publications and TV stations and people wanting to put my mug on advertisements. Or the phone line would ring, and I'd hear, "Come do a talk in Montana." It surprised me, and it continues to surprise me.

I was just trying to win a race, and then all of these people wrote to me saying, "Oh, will you have my child?" Really. I got stuff like that from wacked-out guys. They said, "I have more money than God. Look up my Web site and you can see who I am."

I was invited on the whole dog symposium circuit: Montana, Michigan, Norway. *People* magazine called. *Marie Claire. Cosmopolitan. Men's Journal.* I got the sense that some of them wanted to dress me in a ballroom gown and stand me next to the dog team. People wanted me to become a spokesperson for products. I did that for Outlast Technology, a winter-gear company. I did some product testing for Merrill Footwear. I did some smaller things here and there, for local airlines, little commercials in Fairbanks and Anchorage.

What all of that did was enable us to make the kennel more professional. My life up until then had been working with dogs all winter and then, like most mushers, thinking in the summer, "Boy, I've got to make some money." When all of this started happening to me and money started rolling in, I realized I didn't have to do things the same way anymore. I thought we could really get the kennel on its feet.

My sister, whom we call Kaz, for Kristin Ann Zirkle, helped make the kennel more dynamic. It's now completely computer dependent. When people send you money to support you, they want to see a great Web site and they want newsletters. Now we do that all the time. Honestly, that is not my forte.

Everyone has to have someone guiding him or her in this whole mushing realm. You can't do it yourself and do it really successfully. Either you spend all of your time making money, or you spend all of your time with the dogs. I'm lucky the kennel is on its own two feet; it's run by sponsorships, individuals, small businesses. Fairbanks has been very good to me. I became kind of the hometown girl. People want to be a part of it. People are good.

Winning the Quest in 2000 fulfilled a goal—heck, you've got to come to your goal before you move on—but in 2001 I entered the Iditarod.

The victory in the Quest meant that I wasn't a typical rookie in the Iditarod. People had a lot of expectations; I did, too. I was a rookie in this race, but I wasn't like some people who don't know how to live out there or who aren't going to be warm. I was just exploring a new world.

I never worried about going a thousand miles in the Quest or the Iditarod. But there are huge differences between them. In the Yukon Quest I went for two days without seeing anyone except an official. In the Iditarod a helicopter basically landed on me. There's only one Indianapolis 500, and there's only one Iditarod. You have to be a little more of a showboater in the Iditarod. You have to interact with people more; that's how you're going to get your money. Your capability in the sport is dictated by the amount of money you have to take care of yourself and your dogs. You must appease people who are going to give you the money.

That was a very public season for me, after the Quest win. By August, September, I was back in the thick of it with magazines, TV commercials, and the *Anchorage Daily News* putting me on the cover of their Iditarod section. Musher Jon Little told me that was a jinx.

I wasn't really nervous for the start of the Iditarod, but there is always nervous energy that you and the dogs feel at the beginning on Fourth Avenue in Anchorage. You make sure you don't forget your extra harness, that you don't forget your lead dog.

Basically, that whole fall people had been coming up to me saying it was great what I did and saying they named dogs after me and kids after me. It was nice because the people who are there sincerely appreciate what you do. Most people don't come down to Fourth Avenue on a March Saturday morning on a whim. They come down there to really see why the heck you're doing it and to find out who you are and that sort of thing. Your folks are there and your sponsors are there. It is a big party.

On Fourth Avenue, why not have a good time? The Pioneer Bar is a big sponsor for me. They do a couple of football pools, and I get half the pool money as a fund-raiser. It felt good. It was the beginning of the next step in the evolution of my career.

I wanted to do really well. To me that meant top twenty. I still think that was realistic. I had a really good dog team, which was ready to go. I was ready to go, but I ran very poorly. That's my poorest race. Even on Fourth Avenue I had two dogs coughing. I thought, They're just pulling on their collars too hard, they'll get over it. It's not a big deal, they're just excited. We ran that day, no problem. We spent the night in Wasilla, and there were five dogs coughing and hacking. I was thinking, Maybe it's a minor thing.

The next day those five had minor temperatures.

Pulling into Skwentna after one hundred miles, I could tell that something was wrong. Two more dogs were coughing. The vet put four dogs on antibiotics. It wasn't until after Rohn that I realized the dogs weren't going the speed I had planned. The dogs didn't have energy, and they gave me the biggest reality check to get off my high horse and treat them right then instead of treating my dog team as if it was OK.

Between Rohn and Nikolai, a dog had a seizure and was running a temperature of 105.3 degrees. I thought, Oh, my god. Right then I snapped out of it. I realized I was not racing and that I had better pull the team together or get off the trail. I recognized that everything was falling apart. I was racing, but the dogs weren't. They were trying to, but they couldn't.

I had packed for a twenty-four-hour layover in McGrath. When I came into McGrath, I had two or three dogs in the basket. I had been giving dogs rides; I'd give them a ride and let them out, give them a ride and let them out again. I think I had already dropped five dogs.

In McGrath I gave three vets who were standing there my book, and I said I wasn't leaving until I could leave with a healthy team. It was ridiculous, but I wasn't ready to quit. I declared my twenty-four-hour rest.

It was my first Iditarod; I had to finish the ding-dang thing. The dogs all had fevers. The vets gave them a powerful antibiotic. Eventually, I figured out it was probably an illness they caught from the teams coming to Fairbanks from overseas to train for the sprint championships, a European kennel cough. My dogs probably picked it up three days before heading to Anchorage, exactly the wrong timing.

If I had tapered off a little earlier, I probably could have finished with more dogs. Maybe if I had said I would take an eight-hour rest in Finger Lake or Skwentna. I'd never had a team like that before, and I was really sad. I wanted to compete and I saw all these teams going through. I was there to do well, and it wasn't going to happen.

I had difficulty changing my mindset from thinking I was going to do well to just trying to get to Nome. Between Nikolai and McGrath, I had to decide if I was going to scratch. I had never thought of scratching before; I don't think scratching is good for any dog team. Some people will tell you that it might be the best alternative, but I don't think so. I just had to taper off and fall back, and fall back, and fall back. I left McGrath with nine dogs, and I finished with eight. Basically, the dogs that got me to McGrath got healthy again and got to the finish line. But it sucked.

Every time I came into a checkpoint, the vets knew about me and asked how the dogs were doing. The vets and I worked on it all the way. It was nuts trying to hydrate all the dogs. They had a virus with a fever, and they were coughing mucus. When you have a fever, you have no energy. It was basically sickness, sickness, sickness, and McGrath was SMACK! you're not racing. I had to baby those guys all the way to the end.

It was weird that I ended up with a pack of mushers who at that point weren't really racing. They were out there to have a good time. It was interesting to go from the year before, when I was out to win, to not really racing. In the front of the Quest we didn't even really talk to one another. Now we were saying, "Hey, you want to build a fire? Can I borrow some food?" It had become a trip more than a race.

Toward the end my team was feeling a little better. I pressed them the last 150 miles, and we finished thirty-third. It was not at all what I had in mind. I was disappointed, but there had been the possibility I wasn't going to be able to finish. I am always disappointed when I don't win, but I knew it was a lot better than it could have been.

At the end some of the vets got together and gave me a special award out of their own pockets. That was huge. I learned a lot. I never knew that I could deal with dogs like that. I'd never want to do it again. A lot of people point to sickness as their reason for not doing well in a race. I always looked at them and thought, Yeah, it just wasn't a good race. Well, hello!

I intended to come back to the Iditarod and do well the next year, 2002, but I was happy just to have a kennel and to get to the starting line after Jerry's passing. Jerry was 50 percent of the kennel—monetarily, and in every other way.

He was killed in a car accident on August 3, 2001. He worked for the state Department of Transportation, and in the summer he would do bridge maintenance. He was gone for a lot of the summer. In the winter he worked a week on and a week off, and he would take the dogs up to Bettles. Our whole training and kennel dynamics involved constant movement. He had signed up to run the Quest, and I signed up for Iditarod. One of us would take the A team and the other would take yearlings.

The night of the accident, it was a typical scene where a policeman shows up at your door at eleven o'clock to give you the news. I was not myself for a long while. I personally always have a lot of drive, and we usually started training on August 1. Then Jerry passed away August 3. I had done one run. I didn't do anything for the rest of the month.

People tell you that you're going to become yourself again, but you don't believe it. Then you realize that this is what you do. Mushing was what I did with Jerry as a partner, but it is also what I do. Everyone kept saying, "You've got to do something." September 1, I started training again. We had fifty-two dogs when Jerry passed away, and I gave away twenty in the two weeks after. I couldn't afford them, and I wasn't sure that I was staying in the sport.

I came into the 2002 Iditarod without the high expectations I'd had the year before. I wanted to be happy doing it. I had a bad year dog-wise, too, with injuries and fewer dogs to choose from. The kennel was a lot smaller. I finished in twenty-ninth place.

Now I have the competitive feel back. I started getting out more. I did a lot of talks again—I took all of last year off—and I was surprised when people were calling me left and right again. Come to Maine and do a talk. Come to Michigan, do a talk. Come to Pennsylvania, do a talk. Come to Connecticut, do a talk. I had taken that whole year off, and now I thought, Wow. I started doing the talks, and I like doing it. I like talking to people who are interested. I'm not a preacher. I won't tell you how to mush, but I will tell you how it went for me. I'm not going to tell you that I'm a hundred times better than you are, because I don't know if I am. But I'll tell you what I like do to and why I like to do it, and if you feel like doing it that way, be my guest.

I feel that I am back on track and that things are going well. I know that anything can happen in life, but by golly, I have to just keep shooting straight. Things are going to happen. They'll come up, bling-bling, but I'll deal with them one way or another. I'm not saying my life is going to be a straight line from now on, because that year sucked. That's just the way I have to look at it.

I wake up every morning. It's a typical twelve-to-fourteen-hour day. I'm thawing meat at seven-thirty in the morning, and at nine at night I'm thinking about thawing meat, but for some reason I still like it. I'm not burned out. My kennel is pretty cut and dried. We've got puppies, we've got yearlings, and we've got thirty-two racers in training. We've got five dogs who are retired and who have earned it.

Maybe I'm rejuvenated. Of course I go through the motions every now and then hooking up a team, but then I get out there and see the working dogs and see a dog putting in 110 percent, and I feel guilty that I didn't put in 110 percent.

So the dogs and I really work on each other together.

RACE RECORD

1986	15 days, 9 hours, 44 minutes	31st
1987	15 days, 4 hours, 46 minutes	28th
1991	16 days, 10 hours, 1 minute	28th
1992	12 days, 22 hours, 15 minutes	26th
1993	14 days, 17 hours, 52 minutes	22nd
1994	11 days, 15 hours, 39 minutes	16th
1995	10 days, 23 hours, 51 minutes	18th
1996	11 days, 14 hours, 13 minutes	29th

CHAPTER 13

DAVE OLESEN

Dave Olesen, forty-five, divides his time between two locations in Canada's Northwest Territories. He and his family own a houseboat in the capital city of Yellowknife, but their primary residence is on a remote patch of land on the Great Slave Lake. The closest neighbor is eleven miles away in Reliance. The closest road is 160 miles away.

Although Olesen is usually identified as a Canadian musher, he grew up in Crystal Lake, Illinois, north of Chicago. He was guiding Boy Scout and Outward Bound trips in Minnesota's Boundary Waters Canoe Area Wilderness in the mid-1970s when he hooked up with famed explorer Will Steger, who offered dogsled tours to tourists.

Olesen's long-distance mushing trips penetrated into Canada. He fell in love with the country, bought his homestead in 1985, and in 1991 he became a Canadian citizen, though he maintains dual citizenship.

Olesen, wife Kristen, and their two elementary school-aged girls have a house, barn, shed, sauna, and other buildings, plus twenty-nine dogs, on the property. He operates hardcore wilderness trips for tourists and flies small planes on rural routes for small Canadian airlines.

Olesen considers the 1993, 1994, and 1995 Iditarods his best races, though the performances were wrapped around a depressing tragedy.

Those were great races for me. I was starting to understand the race in a different, more in-depth way. I felt I was racing with people whom I respected and who respected me. Jerry Austin (an Iditarod Hall of Fame member) and I became good companions. Probably the best illustration of that was what happened in 1993.

That was the race that featured the Gang of 17. Jerry and I led that crew into Nome. We rolled into White Mountain, only seventy-seven miles from Nome, late in the afternoon, and a pretty serious snowfall was starting. It was so thick that all we could see were the sled's handlebars. Mushers were there when we arrived, and some more were coming in. In those days they only gave money to the top twenty, so we were all out of the money.

Nobody was getting out. We were piling up there trying to wait out the storm. Over three days it snowed thirty-eight inches. Ketil Reitan said we should just start snowshoeing to Nome. Terry Adkins organized the poker playing and the whiskey drinking. We were having a good time, but we were also eager to get out of there. Jerry was all for punching in a trail. We were making plans to bust out.

Going as a group, that was Jerry's idea. He said, "This is how we should do it." The plan was to take turns breaking trail, then drop back to the end of the line while another musher took a turn. There were seventeen teams. We started out that way, but some of the teams could break trail and some of them couldn't. The notion of this seventeen-team rotation just fell out. A front core of people who had the dogs and were able to deal with the conditions led.

We regrouped in Safety (twenty-two miles from the finish line on Front Street). The whole group assembled there, and we sort of had a round-table discussion. Dewey Halverson said we had the opportunity to make a real Iditarod memory by just piling down Front Street together. It was rare enough to get two teams mushing down Front Street at one time.

The nice thing about the situation was that no money was involved. You wouldn't have had that cooperation. But there wasn't any money at stake, so none of us cared about our place. Oh, some

people said something at first, but they got shouted down.

By that point, I was on a personal high because my dogs had been some of the stars of the show that day. I was so proud, especially of my lead dog, McDougal. It was something to break trail like this in these conditions in the Iditarod, the way we had.

The weather was pretty awful. It was blowing and snowing, and it took us pretty much the whole day to come into Nome. We came in late at night. I was the first one in the group, in twenty-second place overall, and I remember looking behind me and just seeing headlamps strung out. It was quite a sight. Then the street was choked with dog teams, parked anywhere they could find room. I came out of the race with a whole new outlook that year, that I could do well the next year. And then, on November 19, 1993, barely six months later, I lost two 10-dog teams.

We live on Great Slave Lake. We have to wait for the lake to freeze before we can go out to train the dogs. It's the fifth largest lake in North America, so it has to be pretty cold for a while before it freezes thick. That year I made a bad call.

I got out on the ice with the lead ten-dog team. My wife was behind me, following with ten more dogs. I got about a mile and a half out, and the ice didn't seem safe to me. Sure enough, the sled broke through the ice and I went into the water. Just me and the sled, not the dogs. My wife was a ways behind me, and as she approached I yelled for her to let go and jump off the sled, because I could tell she didn't have time to stop it. Her dogs went past me. Then my team pulled the sled out of the water and I was able to get myself out.

It was minus twenty degrees and I was freezing. I had been in water up to my neck. To some extent I regret my actions after that, but I thought what I was suggesting was the best idea. I said to Kristen, "Let's start for home and the dogs will follow us." For a while it looked like it was going to work. The dogs would have a lighter load and the ice might hold.

But then the dogs got farther and farther from shore, and they got tangled up in a big ball in the harness. From twenty dogs all spread out, now there were twenty dogs all concentrated in a small area. It was a thousand pounds of dogs. Kristen and I were almost to shore when we turned back and saw this mayhem of splashing dogs. I was in shock. Kristen said, "The dogs have fallen in." I said, "Get the canoe."

By the time we got back with the canoe, there was nothing moving there. Then we couldn't get the canoe to break through the ice. Kristen jumped out, and she fell in the water. We were both soaking wet, half-frozen. Probably forty-five minutes had passed.

I remember looking down into that hole and seeing a gang line and dogs and black water, and I knew that we had lost them. It was just a horrible event. But it was all put into perspective right after that when Bruce Johnson went out on a training run for the Yukon Quest over at Atlin Lake and went into the water and never came back.

Losing the dogs was a pretty devastating blow for us. But people we had come to know raised money for us. Rick Swenson helped. We leased some dogs and bought some dogs with the money people raised.

I made it back to the Iditarod in 1994, and I finished sixteenth that year. It was my so-called best race. I went all the way to Cripple for my twenty-four-hour layover and won a $3,000 prize. It was kind of neat. People were saying, "Who the hell is that, and why is he is in front?"

I had a lot of fun, but there were no illusions in the minds of the frontrunners, or in my mind, that I might win. There was sort of an acknowledgment that I had taken a token prize. The other mushers had already taken their twenty-four-hour rests.

In fact, I spent more than twenty-four hours in Cripple. When my time was up and I was free to go, it was 11:30 in the morning, the middle of the day, and it was fifty-five degrees. I had no intention of leaving then. I would have to be an idiot to set out with my dogs in that heat and run through the hills to Ruby. I probably sat in Cripple for thirty hours. But the rest did us good. Boy, my dogs just gained momentum after that.

I remember coming into Unalakleet later and seeing mushers all over. There was nowhere to park. I told the checker, "I'm leaving. I'm getting out of here." I just kept going beyond the town, and the team was still good and strong. By the time I got to White Mountain, there was an attraction to being in the money for the first time.

Sixteenth place. That was good. Some of my key dogs had not been lost with the others in the lake. Combined with some of those I bought and leased, yeah, it was a cobbled-together team, but it came together. There were a lot of what-ifs. But it was a fun race. It was a high for me. I was first to Cripple, and I got into the money ($7,746). The team looked good coming into Nome. And I was co-winner of the Most Inspirational Award along with Bruce Lee. It ended up being a great year for me at the finish.

One of the reasons I stopped racing the Iditarod—for now, anyway—is that it was such a logistical campaign to mount just to get to Anchorage for the start every year. I ran the dogs to Yellowknife. Then I loaded up the truck and rolled down the road, where it might break down, and then I drove two thousand miles. Some years I did the John Beargrease in Minnesota first, so I wouldn't even be driving in the right direction to start.

That's what finally did me in. That, and family. It was like this: "Well, honey, I'll see you in a couple of months, and maybe I'll make some money, or maybe not."

I am probably done with the Iditarod in terms of competitive racing, but I don't think anyone's ever really done with the Iditarod. If I don't go back, there are friends in Alaska I won't ever seen again, and that would be sad. The Iditarod becomes such a huge part of your life.

RACE RECORD

1992	14 days, 8 hours, 46 minutes	44th
1993	14 days, 17 hours, 55 minutes	31st
1994	12 days, 13 hours, 13 minutes	28th
1997	10 days, 15 hours, 45 minutes	18th
1998	11 days, 1 hour, 57 minutes	23rd
1999	11 days, 12 hours, 3 minutes	23rd
2000	10 days, 19 hours, 29 minutes	28th
2001	12 days, 20 hours, 21 minutes	37th
2002	11 days, 22 hours, 23 minutes	38th
2003	12 days, 1 hour, 11 minutes	31st

CHAPTER 14

MIKE WILLIAMS

Mike Williams, fifty-one, from the Northwest Alaska Eskimo village of Akiak, is known as "The Sobriety Musher." He has been a representative and symbol of rural Alaskans in the fight against alcohol abuse. Each March, when he packs his sled for the mush from Anchorage to Nome, he includes petitions signed by thousands of Alaska Natives taking pledges of sobriety.

Between 1992 and 2003, Williams transported some 60,000 names—gathered in conjunction with the Alaska Federation of Natives—across the state during his Iditarod races. Adopting the theme of "Take Pride in Sobriety," Williams is dedicated to the effort for deeply personal reasons. Between 1985 and 1996, all six of his brothers died prematurely, from alcohol-related deaths.

His ability to commit to the Iditarod was hampered by finances as he attempted to raise a family, but his anger over the devastation of his people and relatives from alcohol helped push him.

Williams' best finish in ten Iditarods is eighteenth place in 1997. Williams has had more success getting the word out about his higher purpose, traveling extensively throughout the United States as chairman of the Alaska Tribal Council, for the National Congress of American Indians, and as a member of the state board of education.

We grew up in Akiak with dogs. We used them to haul wood and water, and to go from village to village. I was born into this life. We always raced. I started racing in local sprint races at a very young age. In 1973 the Iditarod caught my eye. A psychiatrist friend of mine did a life-stress study on mushers and discovered that those who were the happiest and had the fewest problems performed the best. That was my first contact with George Attla, Rudy Demoski, Herbie Nayokpuk, and Ken Chase, Natives who competed in the early races. It got me even more interested in racing the Iditarod.

My brother Walter did the Iditarod in 1983 and finished thirty-first. It took me quite a few years to get in. Being able to afford it was the main thing. We got a taste of it with Walter, but living in the village, we couldn't get the sponsors. I did the Fur Rendezvous world championship once; Walter did it six times. I got to know the big Iditarod racers: Rick Swenson, DeeDee Jonrowe, and Susan Butcher. They bought dogs from us and we bought dogs from them. Rick kept saying how great the Iditarod was. "Try it, you'll like it," he said. Other mushers noticed what tough dogs we had.

I started mushing for sobriety in the Kusko in Bethel. My brothers Frankie, Ted, Walter, Gerald, Timothy, and Fred, they all perished. These are the six brothers I lost. Accidents. I was sick and tired of my relatives and my brothers dying from alcohol-related deaths. I thought "Take Pride in Sobriety" was a good idea. We have a problem, let's bring awareness to it.

My first Iditarod was in 1992. I started carrying the signatures. I didn't know what I was getting into. Even after all of that time and preparation, I didn't know what the race was all about. I thought I was ready to go out on the trail, but I wasn't. I had a sled that was too small and I had too much stuff. It was the hardest race I ever did, but it was a great trip. It took me more than fourteen days, and I finished in forty-fourth place.

One thing that happened in that race was coming up on Joe Redington Sr. walking along the trail. It was near Puntilla Lake, and he had lost his dog team. I'll never forget the conversation. I offered him a ride, but he said he was sweating a lot already and

would freeze if he stopped walking
and got onto a sled.

It was just great when I got to
the finish line. It was bittersweet.
I thought about my brothers—I
think of them every year when I
finish—and I felt I had accomplished
this impossible thing. I just wanted to
do it once and see how it was, just to
have a good run, just to complete it.
Once I got to Nome I told my wife, Maggie, "I want to do it again."

Since then, it has always been one more time. And each time,
I see changes along the trail: the mountains, the terrain, the people
are always different. I love going to remote areas and going into
Indian country, then the Yupik and Inupiat country. Every year
I've run is different."

When I race across Alaska carrying the message about sobriety,
I think of it as another Serum Run. The Iditarod is connected to the
Serum Run, when mushers brought life-saving diphtheria medicine
to Nome back in 1925. What I do has got to be an analogy with
the Serum Run. Our people are dying from alcohol. I want to go
across the trail with that same life-saving serum. I want to restore
our Native people, to make them strong, sober, and healthy, as they
were before.

Now when I run the Iditarod and go through the villages, I
see changes from ten years ago. They've begun sobriety dances and
parades and other sobriety projects. I keep seeing changes in places
like Nikolai and Shaktoolik. More and more people are becoming
sober, and that's good to see.

People come up to me and say, "Mike, I've been sober for five
years. Mike, I've been sober for three years. Mike, I've been sober
for two years." When I hear those kinds of stories when I'm on the
trail, that really impresses me. We can make changes. We are such a
strong culture. I continue to be bitter about what alcohol has done
to our people, but I'm fighting back. I'm going to continue to do
that as long as I can.

I raced in the Iditarod in 1992, 1993, and 1994, and then I took
two years off. I have five children. I have to hunt moose, caribou,
and black bear and fish in the summer so I can feed them. I have to

fish ten months out of the year to feed my dogs salmon. I have a kennel with fifty dogs, and it is very expensive. I skipped the races in 1995 and 1996. I went to work to pay my bills.

Those two years that I took a break were the hardest two years of my life. I missed the race. When the Iditarod started in March, I couldn't sleep for days. You don't sleep much when you're racing, but this was worse than being on the trail, and I was home in my own bed.

Then I came back in 1997. That was my best run. In 1997 I thought I was pretty prepared. That two-year break gave me the chance to think things over, as well as pay my bills. I think the dogs were better trained. I had more miles on them, and they performed better. I had a great time. I had a real good time traveling with Dave Sawatzky. We raced together for a long time. The dogs seemed to enjoy the run, and I think they could have done even better.

I got off to a good start. I had the least number of problems early in the race than I'd ever had. The dogs were healthy. I think the trail was good. The sun was out. On the run between White Mountain and Nome, that was one of the few times the blowholes didn't blow. You always have to worry about wind there.

At different times I was mushing with Ramey Smyth, Mitch Seavey, Linwood Fiedler, and Dave. We all finished pretty close to one another. They were fast, and I had to work to keep up. It was fun. They'd be there, and the next thing I knew they'd be gone. That helped me. I just kept going with those boys.

Ramey, Mitch, and Linwood all finished just an hour or so ahead of me, and Dave Sawatzky was right behind me. That was my highest finish. My time was 10 days, 15 hours, 45 minutes. I felt pretty good about the race, the time, being in the top twenty. That was a good feeling. Finishing is always a good feeling, but I think it was a good accomplishment. That was my best racing, the best performance I've seen in my dogs.

I think there are several reasons that I haven't done better over the years. I think my stress level has been very high. My brothers' deaths, that's a load in itself. I think I would be way up there if my brothers were alive to help me. I can't afford any handlers. I'm doing everything by myself: training, feeding, and raising the dogs. I'm doing everything.

But I really like being out there on the trail. I do a lot of thinking out there. It's somewhat of an escape. It feels really good to be out there taking care of the dogs, taking care of myself, seeing great country. Physically, spiritually, mentally, and emotionally, it's very good for me.

Even though I kind of go year to year in the Iditarod, I keep coming back. I was going to do it once, but it's sort of addictive. A good addiction, though. If you enjoy dogs and you know what you're doing, then why not do it? I've had a real good time meeting people like Joe Redington Sr. and Charlie Boulding. In 1992 Joe was running a young team, and we were together. We laughed all the way to Nome. Being an Iditarod musher is like being in a club, with everyone sharing an experience. Not everybody does the Iditarod. I've been fortunate to be involved. Each year, I see my friends in Alaska along the trail and in Nome.

People follow you from all over the country. I get a lot of calls and a lot of letters of support. Kids from throughout the country write to me. I answer hundreds and hundreds of letters after the Iditarod. Ten-year-olds from Florida and California and New York know all about my life. Over the years I've been involved, the Iditarod has become quite well known. I feel overwhelmed, big-time.

One of the most important things that keeps me racing is the identification I have with sobriety. If I were racing for glory and money, I could do it physically, but what I have is a deeper focus and reason for doing it. I'm hoping my legacy is that people will remember I did something not for myself, but for others.

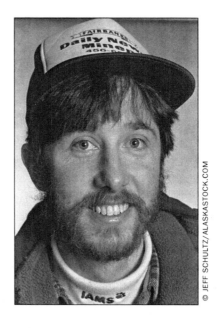

RACE RECORD

1991	22 days, 5 hours, 55 minutes	60th

CHAPTER 15
BRIAN O'DONAGHUE

B rian O'Donaghue, forty-seven, of Two Rivers, Alaska, developed his interest in the Iditarod by covering it as a reporter for the *Frontiersman* newspaper in the Matanuska Valley. Never a full-time musher, O'Donaghue was one of the legion of Alaskans fascinated by the event who dream of trying it some day.

O'Donaghue, now a professor at the University of Alaska Fairbanks, enlisted experienced friends to instruct him and family members to help him financially. In a unique claim to fame, O'Donaghue not only finished last in the Iditarod, earning the Red Lantern Award, he also subsequently raced, completed, and earned the red lantern in the Yukon Quest.

After each thousand-mile race, O'Donaghue wrote a book. He has been known to arrive for book signings bearing a carrying case that holds both red lantern trophies.

As a reporter at the *Frontiersman*, I got to cover the Iditarod. Tim Mowry, now the outdoors writer for the *Fairbanks Daily News-Miner*, and a musher who has raced the Iditarod and Yukon Quest, was the main reporter, and I got to take pictures and write feature stories. Our editor, Shelley Gill, had raced the Iditarod herself, and she stressed that unexpected things always happen to the racers who aren't the leaders.

We approached the Iditarod as a human-interest story and always had fun with it. It was never in my mind to run the race. I just accepted that it was out of reach, financially and in every other respect. But every year I would go home to visit my family back east in Washington, D.C., and I'd bring a slide show of Alaska with me. Just to show my family this crazy place where I was living. Sled dog racing fascinated them all. At a Christmas gathering in 1989, my brother's family made a comment that if I was interested in running the Iditarod, maybe there were ways to make that happen. I just said something like, "Oh, you don't know what you're talking about, but thanks."

Eventually, I figured out that I could do it for $15,000 and I would have to raise $5,000. I had no mushing background. I believe I had ridden with a team, in a sled basket.

But Shelley Gill and Joe Redington Sr. were good friends, and one year when Joe had a team that had been trained for a Russian racer who couldn't get a visa, they put Tim Mowry on a team. With six weeks notice, Tim ran the Iditarod and finished. In a lot of respects, Tim was less prepared than I was. Tim had never camped out in the winter before his qualifying race.

I was living in Fairbanks, but I was covering the state legislature and a special session in Juneau. I filled out my Iditarod application while sitting at the special session, but I didn't get home until July. This was 1990.

I didn't have a dog team. But I cut a deal with a kid down in Knik named Spencer Mayer, who was busy fishing and whose parents were tired of taking care of the dogs. I bought 27 dogs; actually, Tim bought the team and I leased it from him for the purchase price. I got Tim as a coach out of it.

We were living together in Two Rivers, about twenty miles from Fairbanks, and my crash course for the Iditarod began about August 1. I had covered two Iditarods and a Quest, so I had the knowledge about racing that a reporter thinks he has. I had a glimmering of understanding. I didn't have any real knowledge of how individual dogs' talents or aptitudes affect everything, or how the dogs are just not necessarily interchangeable.

To tell the truth, we didn't know anything about the capabilities of these dogs. We never even got to talk to Spencer; he was fishing in Dutch Harbor. We didn't know which dogs were leaders. We tested them all the time. In the middle of runs during the dry-land cart training, we were switching them around. We were trying to find twenty dogs to make a team.

We lost one dog while we were unloading it from the truck in Fairbanks. It took off and we never caught it. We searched everywhere. We always joked that this was the lead dog and we never found it. Never found out what happened to it. It was a chaotic situation. We were putting away a twenty-seven-dog team that we had just transported in borrowed trucks, and the chains weren't rigged right. That was the beginning of my apprenticeship.

We chose the Klondike 200 for my qualifying race because it started in Big Lake and I could see part of the Iditarod Trail. Also, if I blew it there would still be time to enter the Tustamena 200. I did great up to the halfway point. I was in the top ten and having the race of my life.

I hadn't even taken all of our best dogs. I had a team of twelve, and Tim was back in Fairbanks putting mileage on the others. But from the moment I left the halfway point, stuff went haywire. I took the wrong trail out of Skwentna. It was too warm. It was even raining.

At one point, I wasn't cold but my gear was totally soaked. I weighed a ton. I left all of my snacks at Yentna. I got foolishly competitive in the heat of the day. One of my dogs suffered some sort of muscular overheating thing in her hind end and looked bad. I stopped to load her, and I nearly lost the team on an icy lake. I finished the race in disarray and very humbled.

I was twelfth out of eighteen, I think. It was one of my higher placements, but there's a big difference between finishing in organized fashion and straggling across the finish line. I qualified for the Iditarod, though.

I dreamed of being rookie of the year. I thought it was not a crazy thing, though Tim and I would joke that the only way I was going to do well was if an earthquake and an avalanche blocked the rest of the field.

Actually, I thought I would be in the middle of the field. I thought I'd do better than Mowry had; he was forty-second. Then I drew first position. There I was with a team that I thought would roll, and I felt I knew the trail better than some other people did. I didn't expect to be competitive, but I didn't see thirtieth or thirty-fifth as being out of the question, or twentieth, in my daydream. I know better now.

I was going to be the first one out. I was definitely determined that I would stay in front as long as I could, but I wasn't kidding myself that it would be for long. Lavon Barve, a veteran from Wasilla, came up to me and said he didn't want to be rude, but he wanted to tell me exactly how he wanted me to handle my team as he passed. He was starting fourth, and this was at the banquet! Some people thought, "What a jerk," but I didn't. I knew Lavon was a real serious, top musher. And he passed me exactly where he said he would pass me.

People were streaming by me all day. By Eagle River, after twenty miles, I had tumbled major league. I think I was down in the mid-twenties. I know at the restart they said Brian O'Donaghue is in such-and-such position, do you think he can hold it? The color commentator was Bobby Lee, who in later Iditarods was the race marshal, and he said, "In his dreams. He never will."

On the trail out of Knik there was an icy spot, and a lot of teams passed me there. It was a bad spot where their sleds were getting by and hitting my leaders. That didn't really happen with the really good mushers most of the time, but I ended up stopping the sled and running up and protecting my leaders. DeeDee Jonrowe hooked my hook with her sled; I'd probably put my hook in wrong. That turned my whole team inside out with the sled being dragged back toward the dogs. I disconnected the hook, threw it off, and said sorry to people because I was a real bottleneck in the trail.

I started with seventeen dogs instead of the twenty that we were allowed then, and things were going wrong. One dog hit a tree on the way into Eagle River, and I dropped that one. I did feel a bit like George Plimpton, who boxed Archie Moore for a story and played quarterback for the Detroit Lions for a story.

What hope does a reporter have against a professional prizefighter? What hope does a reporter have to suit up and go on the field with the NFL? But mushers come in all shapes and all sizes and all levels of athletic ability. I didn't feel that I didn't belong out there when I started the race. But I look back now, and I didn't know anything.

I eventually got my team straightened out. I found the trail from Knik to Yentna to be really tough. It was so criss-crossed with snowmachine tracks that my leaders were stressed out with a kind of vertigo. I was famished, exhausted, and really thirsty.

Susan Butcher had started about sixtieth, and she just blew by me. Something like forty teams had gone by me, but I thought I was still in the thick of it and I took a nap at Flathorn Lake. It seemed there were a lot of teams there when I went to sleep, and when I woke up it seemed as if hardly anybody was still there.

I had no picture of where I was in the race. I felt a funny kind of disconnect while I was taking care of everything. I was watching, but I lacked that overall perspective of what was happening with the overall flow. It was hard to comprehend how many teams went by during the five minutes I was bent over doing something. When I got to Skwentna, I was second or third to last, and I was shocked to find that out.

I was making sure I was putting the booties on the dogs right, making sure I was taking care of business, that the dogs were watered. I was doing all the things I'd seen people do so they don't flame out early in the race. In that sense, I was still a little cocky about how things were going to work out.

The trail was very rough going into Rainy Pass. The dogs were running through a gauntlet of sticks. I was worried that my sled was going to break at any moment. I don't think I was ever as tired in the race as I was sitting in Rainy Pass. It was in the twenties and very sunny.

John Ace told me that I really should consider moving on, since there was a storm coming. He took off. There is a really steep hill leaving Rainy Pass, and my team hit it and began sliding back. They couldn't get any purchase with their booties on, so I had to take them off and lead my leaders on foot.

I was holding the collar of one of my leaders. The dogs were starting to shake down in responsibilities. Rainy is a tiny dog; she is the one we nicknamed "the lesbian" because of her behavior. I think she weighed less than fifty pounds. Harley is huge. I felt like it was a real accomplishment. Jim Lavrakas, the photographer for the *Anchorage Daily News,* was there. He told me it was a really remarkable scene, something out of the gold rush, because I was pulling the team in front and trusting my sled to stay upright, and the whole team was flattened out against the hill.

It was snowing hard and blowing hard at the top of Rainy Pass. I was depending on Rainy, who seemed to know where she was going, and Harley, who has a big motor and will go anywhere. He's just not very good at directions. I shut down rather than risk going any farther, and John Ace shut down behind me. We zipped into our sled bags to wait it out.

Now, with what I know about a dog team I would have trusted my leaders to take me through it and trusted my ability to stop them on the edge of disaster. I was in my sled bag eating my survival food and thinking, Well, this is the worst thing I could imagine. I was stuck on the top of Rainy Pass in a storm. Joe Redington used to tell stories of being stuck out there when the wind chill was minus-one hundred.

The snow was two or three feet deep in the morning, and I had my snowshoes on, trying to lead my team down the Pass. Lavrakas and Craig Medred, the *Anchorage Daily News* outdoors writer, showed up, and it was like the cavalry. Just passing by, they made tracks we could follow. They could have been Japanese tourists, and we would have cheered. We were looking at a grim situation in terms of how long it would take us to get out of there. I was sinking up to my waist in the snow.

The run down to the Dalzell Gorge after that was beautiful. It was a soft sort of gliding ride through deep powder. We were cruising right on their trail. I had fifteen dogs, but in Rohn, that was the first time in the race where I was in last place. I physically beat five teams into Rohn, but with the time adjustments for the interval starts in Anchorage, I was leaving last by more than a half-hour. The checkers inform you of everything.

I was still continuously ahead of people, and suddenly I was in last place. That did not seem fair. I had to wait an extra two hours.

There was an overwhelming sensation the clock was running, because they were starting to shut down the Rohn checkpoint while I was there. The officials were burning supplies, the tent that mushers can rest in was being stripped down. It was a mass exodus. At that point I was probably two or three days behind the leaders, and I was losing ground massively. It snuck up on me. I was slow getting out of checkpoints. I was sleeping a long time. All of those things are deadly in the first couple days of the race.

Then, coming out of Rohn, I busted up my sled pretty seriously. I had a couple of different accidents. I snapped a small tree leaning in on the trail, flipped over the handlebars, and smashed my headlamp. I had no headlamp then, because when I looked, I saw that the spare in my sled was crushed. The stanchions on my sled were busted, which makes for horrible steering. It was snowing, and I was alone, and I was at the edge of a lake. There was no trace of a trail on the lake. That was the worst moment of the race.

I was worried. I hadn't even crossed the Farewell Burn yet. I wondered how long this was going to take. I was concerned about supplies. I shut down for a few hours. When the light came up, I could clearly see a marker in the center of this frozen lake.

I crossed the entire Burn alone, and the temperature dropped. It was cold. At one point I got the whole team hung up on a stump. The brake caught. I had fifteen dogs ahead of me pulling. I had to cut the stump out; the sled surged, the hook fell, and I leaped on the sled. At another point I went airborne. There were sixty teams ahead of me, and somebody had gone off a little cliff. I followed the tracks, and I didn't realize it until I was in the air and just about ready to come down. I rolled the sled to the side. All of those things made me aware that at any point I could be knocked out of the race. My oldest dog, Skitters, got cut when the sled caught him, a pretty nasty looking cut. A lot of little things were preying on me. And they all added up.

When I got to a creek crossing, mushers Tom Daily and Barry Lee were trying to figure out what to do because it was rushing open water. There were jagged sticks sticking out. Earlier in the day I had seen tracks, and that was an amazing boost to my spirits. One person threw the lead dogs in the water, and the next person drove across. Somebody else was on either side holding the teams. The three of us got into Nikolai together, and we caught a bunch of other teams there.

In Nikolai I got my sled rebuilt. I think I was in Nikolai for fourteen hours, but I was back with other folks, I got some sleep, and I was feeling in great form. I had a great run to McGrath, and I was thinking I was back in the race. Things were starting to click.

In Ophir I just lost my mind. I had to get ahead of people. I was going into the longest run of the race, ninety miles to Iditarod, and I lightened my load and left in the heat of the day. When I look back, I say to myself, "What were you thinking?" Over the next twelve hours, I ran out of food. The dogs were really hungry. Harley, who is about eighty pounds, started dragging us through every camp of every team. Rainy couldn't overpower Harley. He was like a Mack truck. He wanted more food.

For a bit I was off chasing tracks, and they just didn't look right. Later, I was told a caribou herd had been through. Thank god I didn't chase too far. By the time I got to Iditarod, I felt beleaguered and thought that maybe I'd blown up the team. I stayed twelve hours in Iditarod and fed the dogs two or three times.

When I left, the snow was drifting a little and the trail marker situation was going to hell. I re-set some of them for the guys behind me. In Shageluk I stayed with a Native family. That was before the corralling rule. The guy talked to me about his years in Vietnam and being a trapper. The people were just so nice. It was clear in Anvik, but we were antsy to leave because we heard the weather was getting really marginal. Tom Daily and I were waiting for Barry Lee. We tried to persuade him to come with us, but he said, "I just made this run. I want to rest. I'll be with you guys in Grayling." As soon as Tom and I left Anvik, the weather turned nasty. It took us five hours to make an eighteen-mile run. There was light snow, but the wind was just tremendous. We never saw Barry again; he scratched. And Bill Peele, who was back there, scratched.

Rainy and Harley had proved they could go in the wind—a lot of dogs won't—but I didn't think I could break trail out of Grayling. There was another guy there, too, Doc Cooley, who was a trail sweep, sort of the Iditarod representative at the back. We took turns breaking trail and we stuck together. At one point I switched lead dogs, thinking maybe someone else would be better chasing. But the dog balked and those guys disappeared. I felt a real stab of nervousness. In retrospect, I would have let Rainy and Harley lead every step.

We spent two days going to Eagle Island. We were just hammered. There was extreme cold, severe storms rolling over us. We came to a cabin and a person gave us breakfast, and that's where we found out Rick Swenson had won the race. We had 480 miles to go. We came across a snowmachiner, and that was wonderful because now we had a trail. We'd been busting trail—I should say Daily and Cooley were busting trail—and mostly I was grateful that they were there to do it, aware that my race would be over if I was not partnered with the group.

At Eagle Island there were eight other teams. We were psyched; they were more or less scared to leave because of the weather. In the morning, when everyone pulled out we pulled out too. And that group was together more or less all the way to Nome. We were sort of a convoy, though I'm not sure it was benefiting my team. Teams were constantly starting and stopping. People thought of breaking away, but we got more snow outside of Kaltag.

At least, being in this group, there was no doubt I was going to finish, and that was the goal. Of course, I was a prisoner of the worst prepared team ahead of me. It didn't make for the best, fastest, most efficient form of travel.

Not far out of Golovin, I was in the middle of the pack. About fifteen minutes out of Golovin, I realized I had left my parka in the bathroom at the checkpoint. I had to turn the team around. I got into White Mountain with a pretty unenthusiastic dog crew, about 1½ hours behind everybody else. I still had faith I could make that up, but everyone was pointing to the finish line, and we didn't do great coming out of White Mountain.

When I got to Safety, I found out I was 2½ hours behind the next closest team. I was just really, really tired and getting a little discouraged. I was hallucinating too. It came as a shock that I was last; I was fully expecting that someone else was going to be coming in last.

When I started the race, I didn't presume that I was going to be the worst. At Safety, I considered not going into Nome. It was a really low moment. But on the outskirts of Nome, people started driving out on snowmachines and welcoming me. By the time I got to Nome, people were actually cheering. The reception slowly erased all the discouragement.

RACE RECORD

1980	17 days, 6 hours, 50 minutes	22nd
1981	14 days, 2 hours, 47 minutes	19th
1986	15 days, 53 minutes	25th
1987	12 days, 2 hours, 26 minutes	10th
1988	12 days, 4 hours, 21 minutes	3rd
1989	12 days, 2 hours, 6 minutes	6th
1990	12 days, 2 hours, 33 minutes	10th
1991	12 days, 18 hours, 41 minutes	2nd
1992	10 days, 19 hours, 17 minutes	1st
1993	11 days, 47 minutes	6th
1994	10 days, 13 hours, 2 minutes	1st
1995	9 days, 8 hours, 47 minutes	2nd
1996	9 days, 17 hours, 58 minutes	3rd
1997	9 days, 8 hours, 30 minutes	1st
1998	9 days, 21 hours, 47 minutes	7th
1999	9 days, 23 hours, 10 minutes	2nd
2000	9 days, 14 hours, 55 minutes	7th
2001	12 days, 7 hours, 43 minutes	24th
2002	8 days, 22 hours, 46 minutes	1st
2003	10 days, 3 hours, 40 minutes	4th

CHAPTER 16
MARTIN BUSER

Martin Buser, forty-five, of Big Lake, grew up in Switzerland and became an American citizen in a moving ceremony under the burled arch in Nome in 2002. He has won the race across Alaska four times and placed second three times. In 2002 he turned in the fastest race ever, breaking the nine-day (and many say the last) barrier, when he triumphed in 8 days, 22 hours, 46 minutes.

Buser came to Alaska in 1979, planning to stay for a year. He worked as a handler for famed Siberian husky mushers Earl and Natalie Norris and climbed Mount McKinley.

Race victor in 1992, 1994, 1997, and 2002, Buser has won the Leonhard Seppala Humanitarian Award for superior dog care on the trail four times. Buser is married to Kathy Chapoton, a teacher, and his sons Rohn and Nikolai are named for Iditarod checkpoints.

I was introduced to the sled dog world when I was about sixteen and still living in Switzerland. It was a novelty sport in Switzerland. I happened to see a group of people hooking up a bunch of Siberian huskies to a stripped-down, tiny little car—that was their training rig—on a rainy, muddy day. The dogs were excited, and the people were covered head-to-toe in mud, yet they were smiling, having a great old time as the mud flaked off of them.

This was a married couple, and they invited me to go on the next training run. I spent all of my free time with that family. I was a glorified pooper-scooper and did the feeding routine. Virtually all of the mushing was done on carts.

After my military service, I decided to go to Alaska. The Norrises had sold a lot of dogs to Europeans, so everyone knew them. Arrangements were made that I could stay at their house for a year and be an even more glorified pooper-scooper.

The Norrises had raced dogs and won sprint championships many years before, and they were very well known for their Siberian huskies. The funny thing was that when I was flying over the Atlantic, they were going to Switzerland to do seminars. When I got to Willow, there were 250 dogs and the caretaker said, "Here's the truck key and here's the dogs. Have fun."

I barely speak the language—my first language was German—and I've never been in a big kennel. Now I'm taking care of Greenland dogs, Siberian huskies, and some Alaskan malamutes.

I really didn't have any intention of running the Iditarod. Earl had never run the race; he was known to do the speedier races. They liked my work, I guess, and they made it possible for me to run in March 1980, pretty much footing the bill and helping me with all of the provisions. I finished twenty-second with a team of purebred Siberian huskies, and the Norrises made it possible for me to do it again in 1981.

I was hooked and consumed and excited, and ready to strike out on my own. I met Kathy when we were both working at Alaska Children's Services in Anchorage, working with emotionally disturbed kids. I often joke that I was one of her clients. She met me when I was on a dollar-a-day food budget. When I invited her to my house for a dinner date, my food assortment was very limited and very unusual, to say the least. There was beef, fried eggs, and a lot of macaroni and cheese.

When I started accumulating dogs, I made sure they came from proper bloodlines. My foundation was from proven stuff. People don't have a clue. They still think, Well, my dog has four legs and a tail, and it's got a nice coat, so I'll breed it. It's totally counterproductive.

On reflection, I think the second place in the 1991 storm race was sort of a jumping board. My dogs were known for being fast, but it was said that they couldn't handle the weather. We dispelled a lot of those myths and unfounded statements. In 1991 they made it through the weather just fine. This was serious weather, serious enough to turn around mushers with five or six championships who called it impassable. Five of us went in, and two of us came out at the right end.

I gained a totally new respect for the dogs after walking for twenty-seven hours with them, hand-in-hand, being the leader and having the sled constantly blown over by the wind. I was one of those hungry guys who needed to prove something. Not only did I learn about myself, I also really started to understand the dogs and trust the dogs' ability to make it through anything.

My mindset for 1992 was "Never turn back." Every year we make T-shirts, and that was the slogan for the 1992 race. That was the mantra, as we called it. In 1992 the dogs were 2½-year-old seasoned veterans who had gone through storms and had been on the Iditarod Trail.

In 1991 Susan Butcher was totally superior to all of us. We were beat puppies at Old Woman cabin. Her dogs were extremely well hydrated and looked like they had just started the race. I told her I wanted to ask her some things after the race, and she said, "Just let me win this one and I will tell you all." I looked at her and said, "Just let me? There's nothing we can do to not let you win this race." Her dogs were romping and rolling around. Rick Swenson and I just could not believe our eyes.

In 1988 she belittled my dogs and talked about how they couldn't make it through the storm. Then, in White Mountain in 1991, she made it sound like we were the crazy ones for going into the storm. You've got to be careful what you say.

By 1992 I had learned to set up my own schedule and my own race. You have to disregard other people's moves, and you have to be confident that your timing and your strategy are right. I made a move on the Yukon River coming down from Ruby. The dogs were just absolutely peaking. Dave and D2 were the main leaders. I pulled into Unalakleet with seventeen dogs. That's one more than a starting team now.

It was a great-looking team: young, powerful, and energetic. I left Kaltag without seeing anybody. Then Susan, Tim Osmar, and DeeDee Jonrowe had to regroup and start racing one another because first was impossible. And that's how I got such an obscene lead at the finish. I won by 10½ hours. It was the first ten-day race.

It was my ninth Iditarod, and it felt great because I never compromised. I never drove the dogs harder at night than I felt comfortable doing. I raised my own dogs. I never harped on negative discipline; I always harped on positive reinforcement. For a few years there was a lingering question of whether you could win with a soft-hand philosophy. Subsequently, that's the new way. Our dogs run faster, last longer, live longer, and are happier the new way. As a professional dog racer, I think that was the biggest satisfaction, that I never compromised my philosophy. At the finish line, only my dogs and I really knew how cool it was to be there the way we got there.

I won in 1992 and 1994. I was taking turns with Doug Swingley and Jeff King, and when I won in 1997, that victory let me know I could win on the southern route, too.

And then came 2001, when I finished twenty-fourth. People said I was washed up. You hear all kinds of things. People got their jollies by being able to beat me finishing twenty-second or twenty-third. Well, whoop-de-do. Some of my dogs were hurt, and I was physically hurt. I had a bum shoulder. I had a bum knee. I had a cut hand. I had a broken sled. The trail ailments were a hassle, but the overlying problem was the pre-season. We had a horrible training year, and my downfall was that I had gathered a lot of information and data and had started to rely on that more than my intuition.

I have recorded every mile that every dog ever ran out of my kennel forever. I had gotten to the point where the data, the intelligence, was almost running the team by the book. I sort of forgot about the intuition and the closeness, and what had been cherished all of those years: the true camaraderie and intuition that I had with the dogs.

I had gotten too busy and diversified with other things, sitting on the board of directors here and volunteering there, and I was sponsoring a Junior Iditarod team and had a second team in the Iditarod. I had a Serum Run team, and I was doing Rotary meetings, and yada, yada, yada. I didn't see that as a hindrance, because I felt comfortable with all of my data. I was doing my mileage. I was doing the training that the computer spit out over the last fifteen years. I hung my hat on that.

It meant that I was just not focused enough on dogs. I had too much of a shotgun approach. I was doing too many things besides working with the dogs, and they were the ones suffering. My time spent with the dogs was not quality time.

In the winter of 2001-2002, I divested myself of a lot of external commitments. Kathy and I sat down and made a twenty-six-point list of what had to change. What could we do differently? Where did we stray? What happened? At the starting line in 2002, nobody knew what to expect from Martin Buser, including me. But what was different was that I was so relaxed. We worked too hard for it not to be fun.

If you can't find pleasure in doing it, then don't be doing it. The whole season was for joy and fun. We had great helpers, great weather, great dogs, and great training conditions. We did a lot of training that I had never done before. I made more loose runs than ever before, free-running the dogs, camping more than ever before.

That relaxed approach and that relaxed atmosphere helped the dogs go back to my original philosophy. If a guy goes to work happy, he does a much better job. They were so happy. When I took my twenty-four-hour layover in Cripple, it was so cool. I got there first and turned all of my dogs loose. There's not a lot of traffic, and there aren't a lot of people. I stomped out a wider trench than normal. I just flaked out the straw and turned the dogs loose so they could lie wherever they wanted. They could pick whomever they were sleeping next to, and they woke up and went to the sled and stole food and went back to their spot.

The people at the checkpoint couldn't believe it. They would come to me and say, "Hey, you have a loose dog." And I'd say, "I hope they are all loose. I hope they didn't chain themselves up." Linwood Fiedler came in, and then DeeDee Jonrowe and Ramy Brooks, Jerry Riley and John Baker. They were the only other ones. It had to look to them the way Susan looked to us in 1991, in terms of the dogs' energy and hydration and attitude and disposition.

We had no major storms, but we had sixty- to seventy-knot winds in and out of Unalakleet. I broke quite a bit of trail going into Unalakleet, but the dogs were flying nonetheless. I had a good idea and a good plan, and the dogs consistently traveled faster than my projections. In Unalakleet the wind was just ripping. It's good to have a little balance like that. That way nobody can say, "You had all good weather." It was tough getting in and out of Unalakleet.

In 2001 I had stuck it out under adverse conditions. In 2001 there was a lot of wanting to quit, but I couldn't. The two most important reasons I couldn't quit were Rohn and Nikolai, my sons. I couldn't preach for all of their lives that Buser boys don't quit, and then fly home from the Iditarod because I didn't feel good. Also, inside I might feel better for the next two weeks, but I wouldn't have felt better for the next fifty. So scratching was not an option. Sticking it out, just like sticking it out ten years prior to that, boosted my confidence. There were actually a lot of parallels a decade apart.

In Elim I calculated that if the dogs got a lot of rest, they would probably break the record. It sounds counterproductive, but if you rest, you go faster and can achieve better overall time. I forced myself to rest there for three hours. As I was leaving, Ramy Brooks came in and went out. He was going for it, but I had a well-rested team. We talked about it in Koyuk. We sat down together and joked. We both kind of knew each other's moves, like chess players.

It was satisfying in Nome, not just winning but also setting the record. A lot of it was the Swingley factor. People were saying, "What if Doug Swingley had raced?" I got pretty tired of it. My first response to finding out he had dropped back and wasn't racing was, "Well, one down and fifty-seven others to go." It wasn't like the race was over. It was just one competitor who was not there.

There were still plenty of others to worry about.

I kept saying, "What's the big deal? I beat him before he ever won. I beat him in-between his wins, and now I'm probably going to beat him after he wins." Because of all the questions, there was a little bit of extra satisfaction when I got to White Mountain earlier than anybody had ever gotten there before, and with a pretty good cushion. Not only was it going to take away Doug's record, but it also might actually break the last, in my opinion, possible day-barrier.

The eight days will stand. If you're doing mathematical equations, the eight days will stand. Just like the three-something mile will stand. You're not going to have a two-plus-minute mile, and you're not going to have a seven-day Iditarod. People probably said that about eight days, but I don't know if I'm going to live that long for a seven-day Iditarod.

We started the year thinking of a trifecta; I called it the triple crown. I was going to get my citizenship, do the Iditarod, and then snowmachine home to Big Lake. I couldn't know I was going to win and set the record. I mean, Hollywood couldn't write a better script. It's one of those storybook finishes.

We did plan to overlap the naturalization ceremony, and we started in Anchorage. The INS official met me at the start and started the swearing-in procedure, the oath, and gave me the paperwork to finish and sign in Nome. He gave me a little American flag that I stuck in my sled and carried to Nome. Then the naturalization ceremony was completed the day after I won. I ran the fastest Iditarod, but it became the longest-ever naturalization ceremony. That's another record, because they normally last only about forty-five minutes to an hour, and I managed to take more than ten days.

When I first came to the United States, I did not expect to stay. I had all kinds of good job offers in the horticulture field in Switzerland. People thought I was crazy to turn them down. I thought that if I didn't leave then to see Alaska, I probably never would. Those jobs, or different jobs, would be there when I got back.

Instead, I married Kathy in 1983 and became Alaskan and felt very much Alaskan. I could join in with the jokes that we should secede from the union and join OPEC and all of that. Alaska would be its own country. I was perfectly content to be Alaskan with a

Swiss passport. On Sept. 11, 2001, things changed for me.

I go to Rotary at seven o'clock in the morning at the Mat-Su Resort in Wasilla. We had just started the Sunrise Club. On my way, I heard there was an accident with the World Trade Center, a big accident in New York. When the second plane hit the second tower, I turned around and came right home, because it had become clear it was not an accident.

We watched the events unfold on TV, and I said, "This is war, and if I need to fight this is where I'm gonna fight." That was the first time I knew I had to show alliance to the bigger picture. I had represented Alaska at many events. I'd flown to Washington, D.C., and done things for the state of Alaska and felt really proud and very connected to the state. I had traveled to many states representing Alaska and my sport. Switzerland, I knew, would be the safest place if there was a disaster, global war, or nuclear war, but I knew that no matter what happened, that's not where I wanted to be. This is where I belong.

I think the next day I sent off my papers for naturalization, which is a drawn-out process. You have to apply and get paperwork, fill out the paperwork, and go through a bunch of steps. I knew the timing meant that my citizenship papers would probably come through sometime in the winter. Then I thought, No, I would like to be naturalized in Nome under the burled arch.

It was really just a couple of phone calls to make it happen, and everyone was very accommodating and cooperative. Apparently, private ceremonies can be arranged in certain circumstances. The judge in Nome had the authority to do the swearing-in. I was the only one being sworn in, but we made quite a party. It was probably somewhat selfish to want to do it there, but it was good for the Iditarod and it was great for my Nome friends. I thought I had done enough for the race and for the state to be given that little favor. I got it, and I really appreciate it. It was an unforgettable time. Kathy had hats made and everybody had flags. It was just a big celebration. We would have had the same celebration if I had come in seventeenth, but it just happened to be after a first-place finish. That makes the whole story more of a fairy tale.

And then the whole family rode snowmachines the thousand miles home. We took a week and had welcoming committees in the villages. People were looking out for us; the bush pipeline worked.

Talk about a victory lap. We stopped and talked at a lot of schools. The third part of the triple crown was every bit as rewarding and exciting as the first two.

RACE RECORD

1996	11 days, 8 hours, 8 minutes	26th
1997	10 days, 8 hours, 59 minutes	14th
1998	10 days, 4 hours, 54 minutes	13th
1999	10 days, 9 hours, 37 minutes	6th
2000	9 days, 6 hours, 4 minutes	2nd
2001	10 days, 20 hours, 37 minutes	5th
2003	11 days, 8 hours, 51 minutes	23rd

CHAPTER 17
PAUL GEBHARDT

Paul Gebhardt, forty-seven, a carpenter, lives on ten acres of land in Kasilof with his wife, Evy, and daughter Kristin in a house he built himself.

Gebhardt bought his first sled dogs from 1984 Iditarod champion Dean Osmar, and eventually worked with Osmar on his commercial fishing boat, catching sockeye salmon. He bought a remote, five-acre parcel of land thirty miles

north of Talkeetna, built a small cabin there, and trapped the area for lynx, wolverines, wolves, and otter.

Gebhardt hunted moose, caribou, and rabbits for food and sewed hats and mittens out of skins. Kristin was home-schooled. However, he decided that if he wanted to become a serious musher, he had to move onto the road system.

Gebhardt's first race was the Copper Basin 300 in 1994, and he raced his first Iditarod in 1996. His placing improved four years in a row, culminating in his second-place finish in 2000.

I went to my first race with one leader. I had nine dogs, so I borrowed one from Dean Osmar and one from Martin Buser and one from the late Ed Borden. I think I finished twenty-fourth. When I finished, I saw Martin and said, "I never, ever want to go this slow again." We moved up a lot the next year—I was second in the Tustamena 200, so in the winter of 1995 I decided we were ready for the Iditarod.

I thought I had a better team than I had, but I probably had a better team than I showed. I just didn't know how to run them right in a 1,100-mile race compared to a 300. It was a great learning experience. I traveled a lot with Diana Moroney, Dewey Halverson, Bruce Lee, and Tomas Israelsson.

That's the year I saw the polar bear. A lot of people said that the mushers who said they saw the polar bear were hallucinating. The only reason I can say I saw it for real is that Tomas saw the same one in the exact same spot. They put up signs at the Unalakleet checkpoint that there have been reports of a polar bear but no one's seen it, blah, blah, blah. It wasn't a hallucination. We saw it between Unalakleet and Shaktoolik. It was in the Blueberry Hills, about three hundred yards off.

When I saw it, I thought, Those guys hunt people. I had the fastest team of the five of us, and they nominated me to be the back guy. You don't want to put the fastest team in front, because it will walk away from the others. You put the fastest team in the back because it can keep up with everybody. We all had pistols, and I didn't sleep that night.

Only Tomas and I saw it at the time. Dewey was in front, Bruce was behind him, Tomas was next, and then Diana was between Tomas and me. She was having a lot of dog problems at the time, and she didn't see it. Tomas and I saw it at the same time.

We traveled all the way to Koyuk together, and then I got one of those severe depressions that hit rookies. It seemed like the dogs were moving so slow and looked tired. I announced that I was staying there for twelve hours. Those other guys said that when you hit the coast, you don't stay anywhere for twelve hours. They were going to eat and then leave. They woke me up and asked if I was

going, and I said, "No, I'm staying twelve hours, maybe longer."
And I went back to sleep. They took off.

I ended up staying fifteen hours. I don't think I did the right
thing; I think it was a rookie mistake. It probably would have been
better for me all around if I had left with them. But when I went
from Koyuk to Elim, the dogs just flew.

At White Mountain I was two hours behind the whole pack of
them. They kind of hung together, and we had to do our mandatory
rest. My team was looking a lot better, but I had had leader problems
crossing the ice to Koyuk, and I couldn't leave with them.

There was a storm going into Safety. It was wet snow and it
blew into the dogs' eyes. I had to stop and clean it out every fifteen
minutes. It was a side wind and was blowing the team off the trail.
Turning into the Topkok Hills, all of a sudden there was a big wind.
I had my young leaders up there that had never been to Nome.

We came into Safety—we weren't roaring, but we were rolling, at least—and it was a lot nicer there. The other four told the
checkers I had been having leader problems, and they said they had
airplanes out trying to see if they could spot me. I asked when the
others left and was told it was only twenty minutes before. I threw
all of my stuff back in the sled and called the dogs up. I figured we
had just made up three hours. We came over Cape Nome, and I
could see all of those guys strung out. Diana was the slowest one.
I caught her coming onto Front Street.

She let me pass. She didn't have to, because it was no-man's
land, but she stopped and let me pass. I'm not sure if I did the right
thing or the wrong thing. But the dogs made up the time and they
had a great finish. From Koyuk to Nome I made up six hours.

Going through that storm was an impressive thing to watch.
The young leaders had no idea where they were going, but they kept
going to the trail markers. I finally just quit commanding them and
let them go. The best thing I learned out of the whole thing was to
trust my leaders. Martin had been preaching that to me.

I learned how to take care of dogs. I had never run that far. The
dogs learned that there was an end to it and how to deal with it.
But it was a costly learning experience. I didn't have enough money
to buy an airplane ticket. I had to borrow money to get back home
so I could get to work.

After that, I was pleased at how I moved up. In 1998 I was
thirteenth and won the Humanitarian Award, which made me real

happy because it recognized the amount of work I did taking care of the dogs. And the jump to sixth place in 1999 was the biggest thing for me. I didn't think we were ever going to finish in the top ten. That's an elite group.

When we finished sixth, I passed about eleven teams on the Yukon River. I don't know if my guys were going that fast, I think they just stayed steady. Everybody else was slowing down because it was a tough year. I think that's why we could finish second the next year, because I became confident in the team and my capabilities of running them.

The year that I got second, I had four big, strong-headed male leaders that all weighed over sixty pounds. None of them needed a lot of rest, and it rubbed off on the rest of the team. It looked weird. The front of my team was these four huge dogs, and then it kind of dwindled to these little guys in back

The leaders set a steady pace. They wouldn't run fast enough to hurt themselves, and they could go through anything. They would go wherever I asked. If we were going down a hard-packed trail and I said, "Haw," and there was no trail, they went left because they figured I knew a place to go. They trusted me entirely.

I wasn't in front, but I was in tenth or eleventh going into Skwentna. We rested six hours. The weather was a big factor that year. It was getting really hot in the afternoons. We shut down from one to six in the afternoon.

I packed my sled with sixty pounds of food because we had no food drop in Finger Lake. That was probably my biggest mistake in the race. I left at about five in the morning. I didn't want to rest at Finger Lake because the airplanes always land there, but I didn't know if I could make it to Rainy Pass before it got too hot. So I packed enough food to make a nice camping spot someplace.

My team still had fifteen dogs, and we were motoring. I was trying to count how many I'd passed and how many were ahead of me. We rolled into Finger Lake, and Bill Cotter was there. The only guy. It was nine-thirty in the morning, and the air was nice and crisp. We signed in and signed out, and I was in the lead for the first time ever in the Iditarod. That was a good feeling.

You know the song lyrics, "No sled runner track in front of you and no one on your tail?" That was going through my head the whole time. The dog team looked great. I looked at my watch, and I thought we could make it all the way to Rainy Pass before my one o'clock cutoff time. I rolled into Rainy Pass and nobody showed up for two hours. But I carried sixty extra pounds of food uphill for eight hours. Uphill. That was my error.

We rested six hours, which was perfect for me. The dogs were sprawled out in the sun. I pulled into Nikolai, and again we were two hours ahead of anybody else. We maintained this two-hour lead, but I got to hear the media telling me what other mushers were saying: "He don't know what he's doing. He's running way too far." Susan Butcher, who was doing TV commentary, was talking about me blowing up.

Before the race I think people had me pegged as a contender, to get into the top five, but I wasn't a threat to win. So they weren't chasing me. But they weren't going to let me go too far. I never looked back to see who was the next guy coming in. I was looking ahead.

I was on a gut run, on my gut feeling about what the dogs were doing. I watch my dogs and the way they react to what I'm asking them to do, and at that point the dogs weren't reacting like I was asking any more of them than they could handle. Nobody was limping. When I asked them to leave, they were getting up and looking around, alert.

I wasn't laughing about what people were saying, and I wasn't irritated. I just figured that they didn't know my team. I had put a lot of miles on those dogs. We had won the Copper Basin. They didn't have to tell me that I didn't know how to run my dogs. I had run them before, and they were capable of going long distances with little rest. It was the main leaders in front who could do it. They were fabulous.

Red Dog, and Preacher, Plain and Homer. I just rotated those four. Red Dog was in the lead more than anybody. He's bigger and more dedicated than any of the others. When I called Red Dog's name, his ears would go up. Plus, he doesn't need much sleep. There are photos of him sitting in Unalakleet, and the whole team is sleeping and Red Dog is sitting up, waiting, ready to go. He is a phenomenal athlete. That's why he got the Golden Harness Award.

I went through McGrath in the middle of the night, and I won the Spirit of Alaska Award for being the first musher to McGrath. That was a neat deal. It was the first time I'd ever won anything in the Iditarod other than a paycheck at the end.

In Takotna, Ramy Brooks and I were both sick. Nobody else could sleep because we coughed all night. The doctor told me it was a bronchial infection and gave me antibiotics, but they killed my appetite. I called Evy and said, "The dogs are doing fabulous. I'm not doing real great."

I got three hours of sleep in my twenty-four-hour layover. The dogs rested really well and ate great. When I got to Cripple, Doug Swingley had six hours left on his twenty-four. I rested. Martin was around, Rick Swenson and Rick Mackey. Charlie Boulding, Jeff King, and Ramy Brooks went through Cripple while I was there.

I started hooking up when Swingley started hooking up. I figured I would follow him to Ruby. Doug was way faster, since he had just come off his twenty-four-hour rest. I knew Doug was faster. He had faster times between checkpoints. I was running farther and resting less. I caught up to most of the others and came into Ruby third behind Doug and Ramy.

Joe Runyan interviewed me for his Cabela's Web site. I told him my theory was that Doug normally slowed down on the Yukon River and that my team might not be the fastest, but it would not slow down, that we'd just keep moving. I figured if we could pass him when we got to the Bering Sea coast, so be it. Unfortunately, Doug never slowed down that year until after White Mountain. I figured Ramy was out of the picture, because he had run thirteen hours with his dogs and they looked like they had run thirteen hours. On the way to Galena I passed him like he was standing still. My guys were smoking coming down the river. Doug was the only one faster than I was.

When I got to Galena, I had three dogs limping from sore shoulders. The vets said they might recoup in a couple of hours, so we stayed. Martin and Swenson came through and camped at Bishop Rock down the trail with Swingley. Later, Martin and Swenson said they thought I had kind of blown up my team. I stayed four or five hours. I dropped three dogs, but I still had ten and that wasn't bad.

I was watching the clock and realized I could run for eight hours and shut down in the afternoon. I had to run through Nulato and camp later. I picked up straw and food and took off. I was the first guy at Nulato. I was surprised. I was leading. I saw Swenson and Buser, but I didn't see Swingley. I said, "Where did Doug go?" They had no answer. Later, I saw Doug on TV when they told him I had gone through. He said, "He wouldn't have got through here first if I hadn't overslept."

Doug came up on me about half an hour before I was ready to camp. That team, I could see why he won. They were loping out on the river. They got film of it on the Iditarod video. When he's coming up, he's loping and I'm trotting with a bale of straw. See you later.

I was having a fun time. Swenson was totally scratching his head because he couldn't figure out how I was running. And Swenson's a master at figuring out everybody else's schedule. I just laughed. At that point I didn't care where I finished. I was racing with the big boys and playing their games and making up my own schedule.

Coming into Koyuk at dawn, my ten dogs were motoring. You can see the Koyuk lights forever going across the ice, and I thought Doug might still be there. So I shut off my headlamp. I came to town, and there was Doug just hooking up his tug lines. Red Dog was a couple of feet from him when I turned on my headlight.

I hollered, "I'm going straight through." And Doug was acting as if he was thinking, "I screwed up. I waited too long." He was pushing to get out of there. I stopped and loaded some food and got out about ten minutes behind him. But I never really saw him again. He zoomed away and we camped right before Moses Point for four hours.

When I got to White Mountain, I was five hours behind Doug. He was not slowing down at all. I didn't figure I could beat him unless he screwed up, but I wanted to stay within striking distance. I told the guys at White Mountain, "Unless he falls in the ice or something, I can't beat him." But I didn't want to just concede. I also had Jeff King coming up behind me. I didn't want to lose second place. I thought that was a pretty spot.

I only lost about four minutes to Doug from White Mountain to Nome. Finally, I got the equal speed he had, at the end of the race. When I got to Nome, I was ecstatic. Doug finished in 9 days, 58 minutes, which was a record at the time. I finished in 9 days, 6 hours, 4 minutes. At the time it was the fifth fastest Iditarod ever. I was in pretty good company. I was totally on cloud nine.

That was the most exciting race I've ever had. That was the only race I ever led that much. I know I can win. I proved we can win. I think when I trained Red Dog I instilled that into him, that we can win. Whoever finishes second is capable of winning. So it's just a matter of everything having to be just right. It may never happen, but it may. It's possible.

RACE RECORD

1984	15 days, 15 hours, 29 minutes	27th
1987	12 days, 9 hours, 13 minutes	14th
1989	13 days, 10 hours, 34 minutes	24th
1990	14 days, 22 hours, 23 minutes	28th
1993	14 days, 17 hours, 54 minutes	26th
1994	11 days, 17 hours, 21 minutes	19th
1995	Scratched	
1996	11 days, 8 hours, 10 minutes	26th
2000	11 days, 5 hours, 14minutes	31st

CHAPTER 18
DIANA DRONENBURG MORONEY

Diana Moroney, forty-seven, of Chugiak, grew up in California, where she was studying to become a lawyer when she received a phone call offering her the chance to move to Barrow, Alaska, as an expediter. She didn't know what an expediter was, and she didn't know where the northernmost settlement in North America was without looking a map, and she had to make a decision within twenty-four hours. She took the job.

She arrived in Alaska in 1976 for a six-month job and stayed. She started mushing when she and her first husband bought a five-dog team from a dog driver in the Matanuska Valley. Moroney was five months pregnant with her son John when the dog team arrived by air, accompanied by a piece of paper that provided the dogs' names, positions in the team, and instructions on how to attach them to the gang line. She learned to hook up a team by trial and error.

The dogs were used to regular, tree-lined trails and had never run on tundra, so they ran all over the place.

After leaving Barrow, Moroney fell in love with the Iditarod. Her first race was in 1984, and she met her second husband, Bruce Moroney, through the race. In years that she does not race, Diana Moroney, a professional pilot, flies the trail as a member of the Iditarod Air Force.

Mushing in Barrow, the dogs zigzagged all over the tundra. My husband, Ray Dronenburg, didn't want me to mush because I was pregnant. I made a deal that if I fell off the sled, I would stop. The very first rule you teach rookie mushers is never to let go of the sled, because they will lose the team. But if I didn't let go I would have fallen. So I just let go. The dog team found its way back to Barrow, and I just hiked back. People were constantly calling Ray saying, "Here comes Diana's dog team." He said, "That's OK. She'll show up pretty soon." It worked out. I never fell. This was in 1981. It was wonderful.

I had no clue, nobody to guide me, absolutely no idea what I was doing. One day one of the leaders, Pepper, just stopped and did a 180-degree turn on the sea ice and started coming back. I said, "I don't think so." I lined him up and said, "Let's go." And he did it again. This went on for half an hour. I couldn't figure out what he was doing, but I wasn't going to let him win.

I was absolutely flustered. I turned them around, and the dogs took off like bats out of hell. Everything was fine. When I got back to town, I realized he was basically protecting me. Not far down the trail they were blasting. The dog knew it and wasn't about to go through there with me on the sled. Pretty good little dog. I figured out if a dog doesn't want to do something that badly, maybe there's a reason for it.

By the time we moved to Willow, we had fifteen dogs. We started doing sprint races at Montana Creek. We met a lot of other mushers, and it became more fun to do distance training. Ray ran the Iditarod first, in 1983. The first two-hundred-mile race I did started in Montana Creek, went to Skwentna, and came back, and it took me seventy-six hours. It was won in fifty-something hours.

The next year, we became the first husband-and-wife team to do the Iditarod. I trained the teams because Ray was gone a lot to work. I was in the top thirty going into Finger Lake, but there was three feet of fresh snow and I couldn't find Finger Lake. Going into Rainy Pass, I turned to Rick Mackey and asked, "Is this the hard part?" He said, "Nope." It started raining, and I never did see the hard part there.

When you take off out of Rohn, you go up a creek bed. Normally it's frozen, but instead it was a streaming, flowing creek. The dogs kept trying to jump into the trees. The trail was on deep water. And then there was pure mud, not the slightest trace of snow. I was thinking, This is the Iditarod?

I was wearing a pullover parka, wool pants, bib pants, a beautiful wool sweater, a pullover sweater that my mother had knitted for me, and I was dripping wet. Anytime I had to pee, it was a nightmare because everything had to come off. It was the worst experience of my life, getting through that Iditarod—and it was fun.

At one point I was following Gordon Castanza around the edge of a lake and I thought things were wonderful. All of a sudden his dogs turned right and headed into the water. I stopped and thought, No way. Then I could see other teams ahead, and there were about seven teams going through a foot or so of standing water.

I had this little, bitty thing of a leader named Dolly. I told her to go, and she looked at me as if to say, "No." I picked her up and tossed her in the water, and on we went. We had the big old toboggan sleds, and they kind of floated on top while we ran alongside. It looked like we were walking on water. A little later down the trail it got colder, and by the time we reached McGrath it was minus-forty.

I hadn't studied the trail, and coming out of Unalakleet, I couldn't find Shaktoolik. I thought, Where is this Shaktoolik place? It's gotta be around here. It was getting pretty stormy. It was just really tough going. When I got to Shaktoolik, I was absolutely depressed. When I walked into the checker's house, there were Sue Firmin and DeeDee Jonrowe and Rick Mackey. I thought, What's he doing here? He won the race last year. That's when I realized I must be doing better than I thought.

Coming up Front Street in Nome was the most exhilarating feeling in the world. I finished the Iditarod, ending up twenty-seventh. I've finished eight out of nine Iditarods, and what surprises me each year is that I still get that same feeling at the end of the trail. I get all choked up with tears. The feeling has never wavered.

I would do it every year, but I can't afford it. I don't have the money for a handler, and I have to work. I commute to Nome. I travel to work a week on and a week off, and I fly for a living. When I fly for the Iditarod Air Force, I take supplies into the remote checkpoints, hauling straw and musher food. Once the race begins, I haul dropped dogs, vets, checkers, and race judges. I've done that three years. I've also been a checkpoint coordinator. Bruce is a pilot, and he flies all over the world out of Anchorage. We had a flight school, but we shut it down. He flies for Atlas Air Cargo. I fly for Arctic Transportation Services.

Bruce and I met through the Iditarod. We were both flying, but we were barely acquaintances. One year I worked as a dropped-dog coordinator while he was working as an Iditarod pilot. We briefly passed in the halls at race headquarters.

In 1992 I was doing the Hope event, the race to Siberia, and I was in Nome and went to the finishers' banquet, but I didn't really feel part of the Iditarod. A friend suggested we go out for a beer, and two guys walked in. One was Glenn Hanson, and I said, "Finally, somebody I know." The other was Bruce. We went out drinking and dancing, and eventually I said I had to go because I had to get ready for this race. Bruce asked me if I needed any help.

He helped me out all day in return for a dogsled ride. He had never been on a dogsled. I told him I would meet him at a corner and slow down, and he could just hop onto the sled. Well, this was a young team and it was real crazy. It didn't work. I ran over Bruce. The dogs just flipped him right over and I kept going, yelling, "Sorry, I'll be back."

I had fourteen dogs and couldn't slow them down. I was a couple of miles out and headed toward Front Street. The dogs were running full bore because they hadn't run in a couple of days. I flipped the sled over and I was dragging on it, trying with all of my force to stop it and get them off the road, and it wasn't working. Barb Moore was driving up the road and saw me, and helped me get the team off the road. She asked, "What are you doing?" I explained that I was supposed to give Bruce a ride, but I had left him and could she pick him up. She did, and we went for a ride and he had fun.

Then I went to Russia. He ended up coming over to my finish in Russia, and I thought, This is a guy I've got to keep around. I ran the Iditarod in 1993, and Bruce decided he wanted to try it. I told him he could take the puppy and old fart team and a bunch of borrowed dogs in 1994. I trained him and the dogs.

That was the year of the "gas-house five," the mushers who got caught by propane fumes in a tent at Finger Lake. I had been in that exact same tent with other mushers, but the flap was always open, letting in air. I couldn't sleep, and I remember standing over the heater with a headache. It was probably because of the fumes. I held my hands over this propane heater, and I never even noticed it wasn't vented through the roof.

We left, and the back of the pack came in: Bruce, Lisa Moore, Mark Chapoton, Catherine Mormile, and Jamie Nelson. They decided they were going to spend the night. Bruce's idea was to run during the day, sleep at night, and enjoy it. He was not going to compete.

Well, Jamie Nelson woke up and couldn't wake anybody else. Beth Baker, who is a doctor, was sleeping outside on her sled, and Jamie came out hollering and screaming that there was a problem. She was getting sick and couldn't wake anybody else. Beth apparently recognized the problem, and they pulled all of those guys out of the tent and threw them in a snowbank.

Bruce said he remembered being woken up and slapped around. He said it was the worst two-bottle gin hangover he'd ever had and that he felt horrible for days. The Iditarod wanted to pull them out of the race. They wanted to continue, but they made a deal to stay put for twenty-four hours.

I had been in Rohn when they knew about it, but they weren't sure the mushers were going to survive, so they were trying to get me out of Rohn when this stuff was coming over the radio. In Nikolai one of the race judges, Andy Anderson, came up to me and said, "Diana, I have some news for you. I have to talk to you." I said, "Is Bruce OK?" That was my first knowledge of the gas incident, but they patched me through to him on the phone and I talked to him.

That incident kind of goofed up Bruce's plans. He kept asking me where I was going to take my twenty-four-hour layover so he could catch up, and I kept telling him I didn't know, that it depended on the race.

I told him I was set up for Nikolai, McGrath, Takotna, or Ophir. He said, "I hope you take it in Nikolai. Then I'll be able to see you." I said, "Bruce, once this race starts, don't get mad at me if you never see me." I was racing pretty well and I finished nineteenth. His idea was that he was going to push until he could catch up to me on my twenty-four and then propose marriage. But the gas ordeal put a stop to that.

Instead, Bruce enlisted some help from Tim Woolston, a reporter for KTUU-TV. There was no taping, nothing pre-arranged. Bruce said, "Why don't you just start the camera?" It was all ad-libbed. They taped Bruce working on his dog team and doing stuff and talking, and next thing you know, he was on the runners of the sled, proposing to me by video.

That was before my finish, and they kept it hush-hush. But Jack Niggemyer, the race manager, started spreading rumors around town, so a lot of people came out at 2 AM. Before that, though, I had a big problem in Unalakleet. I had a dog that was just doing this horrible, projectile vomiting. I thought he was going to die. I dropped him, and it turned out it was an ulcer. I was not in a good mood. And then Tim Woolston came running up after flying ahead on the trail from Bruce.

He started interviewing me about the race and my plans at the finish. He went on and on. Anyway, as I was going into Nome I could hear on the radio someone talking about something special for a musher and blah, blah, blah. I started to think, "All right, what's going on?"

In Safety I had a problem with a really good leader named Nuka, who was acting up. I was really ticked and I talked firmly to him. Then, in Nome, race marshal Bruce Lee said there was a protest filed against me and I had to come see a video. My mind blanked. Did I do something wrong? They took me to the finish chute, and on a tiny little TV they started to show me this footage.

And then it came on. It was Bruce proposing, and I started laughing. He asked if I would marry him, and I said, "Yes, of course I will." He wouldn't have done it that way if he wasn't sure. It turns out the video clip was on CNN for days. People saw us overseas. A friend of mine was in Japan, and he saw it. I couldn't believe it.

We got married in June in Anchorage. KTUU sent a reporter to the wedding and taped that, too. I really wanted a church wedding. I had a big, white gown and my old leader, Ruby, was there. Everybody said I had to get rid of the dog, but I said, "This is not a dog." I went into Rae's Harness Shop and saw Pat Rae and said, "Pat, do you have any bridal harnesses, by chance?" Pat made a beautiful white harness for Ruby. And she walked with the ring bearer.

In 1997 this gal named Danielle Thomas contacted me. She was a writer and was married to the famous novelist Wilbur Smith, who writes adventure books. She was going to write a book that included the Iditarod, and she came out from England and flew the trail with a friend for three days. They couldn't believe this place.

We sat in the cabin in Rohn and I told her Iditarod stories. It was really neat. All of these things would come back to me. The book is called "A Far Distant Place." She used our real names, Bruce's and mine. It's basically a love story about this gal in Barrow who runs the Iditarod. She leases the team from Diana Moroney, and Bruce Moroney teaches her to fly.

I couldn't figure out why I never heard from Danielle, because I knew she would send me a copy. I finally got an e-mail from her friend about something else, and I wrote back and asked if the book had never gone to the publisher. The friend thought I knew. Danielle Thomas died a week before the book came out. I presume of cancer. I think she was ill when she was in Alaska. I finally found a copy of the book on the Internet.

Once, at a presentation I gave, somebody asked if I like flying the trail better or mushing the trail better. I said, "When I'm flying the race, I look down and wonder why I'm not running the race. And when I'm running the race and I see the pilots go overhead, I think, "God, I wish I were up in that plane right now, flying."

RACE RECORD

1983	15 days, 10 hours, 40 minutes	28th
1984	14 days, 3 hours, 55 minutes	11th
1985	18 days, 14 hours, 55 minutes	6th
1986	13 days, 15 hours, 29 minutes	16th
1993	11 days, 13 hours, 4 minutes	11th
1994	11 days, 11 hours, 34 minutes	13th
1995	9 days, 20 hours, 5 minutes	8th
1996	10 days, 59 minutes	9th
1997	9 days, 20 hours, 58 minutes	5th
1998	9 days, 22 hours, 40 minutes	10th
1999	10 days, 6 hours, 25 minutes	3rd
2000	10 days, 5 hours, 34 minutes	21st
2001	11 days, 18 hours, 57 minutes	11th
2002	9 days, 7 hours, 47 minutes	5th
2003	11 days, 5 hours, 37 minutes	21st

CHAPTER 19
VERN HALTER

A native of the rural farming country of Flandreau, South Dakota, Vern Halter, fifty-four, of Willow, Alaska, trained as a lawyer, and after coming to Alaska in 1977, worked at a Fairbanks law firm and served as a magistrate in Dutch Harbor in the Aleutian Islands.

Each year, after the Iditarod, Halter spends about six weeks showing mushing videos and lecturing to school groups in the upper Midwest, visiting sixty-five to eighty schools each spring. He estimates he has talked to almost 300,000 students, and he hopes one of them grows up to become an Iditarod musher.

Halter and his wife, Susan Whiton, a two-time Iditarod musher and a veterinarian, operate the seventy-five-dog Dream A Dream Dog Farm. His best Iditarod finish is third, in 1999.

The listing of my homes in Alaska for my early Iditarods is kind of funny: Unalaska, Dutch Harbor, Moose Creek, Trapper Creek, Kotzebue, Willow. I lived in Kotzebue for six years. From April to Halloween I was a public defender. Then I brought all of the dogs to the Matanuska Valley to train. I always liked Dutch Harbor better, but my mailbox number was actually Unalaska. Moose Creek should actually be Trapper Creek. I still own the five acres in Trapper Creek that I started out on in 1980. I basically have always trained out of there, even though Willow is my box number now.

It took a long time before I shifted from just trying the Iditarod to giving up my law work. Winning the Yukon Quest in 1990 got me a sponsor. I picked up a really good commercial dog food company because of that. The Quest is a tough race, and in 1989 Jeff King beat me. To come back and win was fun.

To tell the truth, the reason I was in the Quest was to improve my ability with dogs to go back to the Iditarod. Winning was just gravy, icing on the cake. Susan was finishing vet school at the same time. She was going to Washington State, and I was trying to put her through. Then I went full-time into the racing kennel. I got lucky: I got in with Norwest Bank in South Dakota, Minnesota, and North Dakota, and they merged with Wells Fargo, and I got a dog food sponsorship. That was a critical time for me, 1989-1992. It allowed me to race all the way up to 2003.

I've had a lot of high finishes in the Iditarod, but I can't seem to figure it out. On the Yukon Quest I got in there and had focus: second, third, first. The Iditarod is so much more complex, and there are certainly more competitors. The Iditarod keeps getting away from me. It gets away from me and I just play catch-up.

I think it's me personally, my personality. The last couple of years I think I've gotten better focus and a little bit more drive. I don't have that many more swings at the plate. That was a very talented dog team that was fifth in 2002, but I think it had more talent than that. I think I've had a lot of talented dog teams with a moron on the runners. I think some people could have taken these dog teams and won.

The 1992 Iditarod team should have won. I was seventh, but that was a heck of a dog team. That was one dog team that I will always remember, and probably one of the greatest dog teams I've ever driven. I had a full twenty dogs that were really good. It was just a sensational team.

Some years I am pretty confident going into the race, and I usually get blown away those years. In 1999 I had no particular aspirations. I really had a nice dog team, but the dogs were old. I wasn't quite sure where they would be. But they kept getting stronger and stronger. The dogs were seasoned, and they kept their speed up. I started the race very methodically. I didn't care where any other mushers were. I just set a pace and gradually started increasing it. I think the dogs gained a lot of confidence, and so did I. When I started asking things of them, they were ready.

They could go seventy-five, eighty-five miles, and it didn't faze them. They just looked great. About five hundred miles into the race, I was in twenty-eighth place but I knew I had a good outfit. Bruce Lee, the musher, was a race judge that year, and he said, "You know, I haven't seen any dog teams like this around here."

I started moving, taking long, fast, hard runs, and it wasn't fazing the dogs. At Eagle Island I got a really good look at Rick Swenson's team. He was eight hours ahead of me, and I started to think about trying to run him down, an hour or two each run. I passed him out of Elim, and that was so much fun to pass someone like him.

Before that, I had passed a lot of teams. I got a lot of them right away, right out of Iditarod going to Anvik. A lot of teams on the Yukon River were starting to falter a little bit. I was really pulling away from those guys.

Charlie Boulding, Paul Gebhardt, Jeff King, John Baker, they were all around me, but I had those guys under control by Kaltag. I could see them, but my whole idea was to focus on something ahead of me. If you keep your focus on something behind you, you're going to mess up. If you're just trying to stay ahead of somebody, it means you're either weak or thinking about the wrong thing. I had more power and speed than they did.

I never could close on Doug Swingley and Martin Buser. There was a big gap that year between first and second and second and third. But I was extremely happy when I got to Nome. Every time I get to Nome, it's a great feeling to me. I don't care what position I'm in, I really did something with a dog team and performed really well. But 1999 was an exuberant year. And it was the last hurrah for that dog team.

I did a classic thing a lot of coaches do: I hadn't been working on my young ones. I'd kept that seasoned team together, and those dogs gave me that one last great feeling. They were all seven, eight, nine, so I had to enjoy it while I was there, at that moment. Two years later, 2001, I was twenty-first because I had all these young dogs and was rebuilding. And they were sick.

You need one of those finishes every once in a while, just to let you know that things aren't perfect in the sled dog racing world. It reminds you that it's volatile, that if you're not working as well as you should be, things like that can happen real easily.

I just got complacent. I think that finish was really a kick in the pants to get going again. The next year, I was eleventh, a better performance, but it still wasn't the level of the dog team. I wasn't really dissatisfied, but I knew there was work left to do. I cut the kennel in half. I used to have a hundred dogs, and now I keep forty-five or fifty. I had too many dogs, average dogs, and I needed to put in the labor. I thought that if I spent more time with the top dogs, maybe that would be the thing.

The best thing I did was to make an age chart. I had that for eight-year-olds, five-year-olds, and four-year-olds. All of a sudden I thought, By golly, I don't have any two-year-olds, and I knew I should purchase some. Having dogs of all ages and keeping an eye to the future is important.

When I first did the Iditarod, I took any dog I could get. I'd borrow a dog, put it in the team, and if I worked hard and fed a pretty good diet, I'd probably be in the top ten. There are young people who are figuring it out real quickly, and they put a lot of pressure on you. If you're not ready, they're going to beat you.

We've got some pretty good young mushers, but we don't have enough of them. It takes so much money and capital to own dogs, to have facilities, doghouses, dog food, and labor. It's just like farming. It takes years to own the farm: buy it, pay for it, have the land.

In 2002 I felt great. I had worked out with a personal trainer, and I knew my team was good. A trainer makes you work a little harder. If you go to a gym yourself, you'll lift some weights and get on the treadmill. But a trainer will make you push it. Trainers get to know you, where your weaknesses are. DeeDee Jonrowe is at the upper echelon of mushers as far as physical training. She's been a marathoner, worked out with weights. She's a great lady for that. It takes a lot of drive—time and motivation.

I don't know if I am in better shape than I was twenty years ago. You always hear that once you are over fifty, you don't recover quite as quickly. If you're out of shape, that really emphasizes the lack of ability to recover. And the key to being a good musher is to recover when you get your chance to. If you don't, then you're just going to deteriorate along the trail. I would hope I'm going to get two hours of sleep a night. I think I almost have to, to perform well. Three would be better.

Physical conditioning helps best with sleep deprivation. Your muscles recover quickly, so there's less stress on your body. You hold up mentally, you can perform physical tasks better and faster, and you get injured less. Your chance of injury or stiffness or soreness is going to be a lot less. I still think I can win the Iditarod. I guess I've never had a performance where I've shown what I'm capable of, but I still think I can do it. Forty to forty-eight is probably a terrific age range for the Iditarod or the Quest. It's a combination of experience and background and physical ability. You can extend that if you work very hard. I'm trying to extend it a couple of years.

I also tried to put a tremendous amount of muscle mass on the dogs during the 2002 training season. I kept them on four-wheelers with bigger teams. I used twenty-two dogs, pulling a tremendous amount of weight for a long period of time. It was time on their feet. I used to do it a lot in my Yukon Quest days and got away from it. And then I cut the number of dogs in half, doing fifty-, sixty-, sixty-five-mile runs in pretty quick times. It paid off big time. The dogs had great muscle tone.

Early in the race quite a few teams passed me, but later on in the race it seemed as if my dogs could go by anybody. They really held their quickness. On the starting line, after being twenty-first, then eleventh, and changing things, I was scared to death. I was pretty confident that the dogs looked good, but you never know.

In the early going I was in a lot better place than I normally am, maybe two, three hours behind the leaders. I took my twenty-four-hour layover in Takotna, and I was well positioned. Going into Cripple, the leaders were there. I went straight to Ruby, and I think I had the fastest time. Everybody was all around me. Martin Buser was there. Ramy Brooks was there. DeeDee was there. John Baker was behind me, but I didn't even realize it and he went on to get third.

They all skipped Galena and went another twenty miles to make camp. I stayed in Galena. I was the classic "wuss" machine; I was being conservative. But that dog team should have gone down the trail with the others. I thought maybe I would gain an advantage in rest. I had straw there, food—I could really refuel. I thought I would be able to just go in and out of Nulato, but it warmed up to forty degrees. I had to run the dogs in the warmest part of the day, so I had to stay in Nulato for six hours to avoid the heat.

I ended up fifth, but it was very satisfactory. That was really the goal, to be in the top five. It was really pretty good to see the changes pay off. It made me pretty excited for the future.

The dog team is there. The equipment is there. The knowledge and ability are there. It's just a matter of strategy. Doug Swingley is the oldest person to win the Iditarod. He was forty-eight when he won his last title. I want to be the oldest person to win the Iditarod. That's exactly my goal. I've never given up on it.

For me, winning once would be all that I need. You would probably see the retirement sign out real quick. Well, maybe not. I really enjoy sled dogs and the training. I think winning would be fulfillment. It's always nice to see your dog team be the best. That would be really fun for me. That would signal something for our kennel.

RACE RECORD

1999	12 days, 20 hours, 53 minutes	36th
2000	10 days, 7 hours, 44 minutes	23rd
2001	11 days, 23 hours, 46 minutes	15th
2002	9 days, 7 hours, 22 minutes	4th
2003	10 days, 15 hours	13th

CHAPTER 20
JON LITTLE

Raised in the Seattle suburbs, a graduate of the journalism program at Northwestern University near Chicago, and a full-time reporter when most top mushers don't have time for jobs, Jon Little, forty, of Kasilof, Alaska, might be considered an unlikely dog driver.

As a college student, Little harbored fantasies about becoming a bush pilot in Alaska. He answered an ad for a newspaper reporter at the *Peninsula Clarion,* and that brought him to Alaska in October 1987.

Iditarod racer Tim Osmar gave Little a leader that couldn't make the cut in his race team. The dog, named Manley, was a female that Little called the manliest dog in his yard. Little began taking runs out of his yard, and that led to racing.

In 1999 Little entered the Iditarod for the first time, placing thirty-sixth. Over his next three races he exhibited phenomenal improvement, finishing fourth in 2002. It was a remarkable achievement for a musher with somewhat of a shoestring budget who operates a small kennel.

Igot into mushing after hanging out with some friends who handled dogs for another musher, Tim Moerlein, who raced the Iditarod in the 1980s. Then I got dogs from Tim Osmar. I just liked going on the trail.

Even back in 1994, I would buy gear from time to time, just in case I could wear it in the Iditarod someday. I was thinking ahead to the Iditarod, but I wouldn't tell anyone that. I was afraid they were all going to laugh at me. I had a mediocre team, and it seemed like I had a long way to go to even have a quality dog team.

Tim Osmar was actually one of the first people who noticed that my team was getting a little bit better. At one race he said that I had more power than I knew what to do with. I had maybe twelve dogs.

When the *Anchorage Daily News* hired me in 1995, I moved to the Matanuska Valley, about fifty miles north of the city. Musher Lynda Plettner had a cabin on her property and I stayed there. I was on the copy desk, and I commuted an hour each way to work. I could run my whole team with one workout then, and not have any left over.

The job on the Kenai Peninsula opened up in 1997, and my dog kennel grew quite a bit. I started buying dogs from Dave and Dana Scheer; they were going through a divorce. I think of them as the Lennon and McCartney of local mushing. Most of my bloodline came out of there. I even moved into their house.

One of the things that helped me out in my first Iditarod was the loan of a dog named Kazan from Dana, who thought she would become a good leader. I bought Kazan, and she has been the basis of my team ever since. She's just a great leader.

I entered my first Copper Basin 300 in the late 1990s. That was an eye-opener. The most I had done was a two-hundred-mile race, and this wiped me out. I was dehydrated and hallucinating, and I really did a horrible time, but the team ended up marching to the finish line in thirteenth place.

I just didn't know how to take care of myself. I didn't understand that if you don't drink frequently, really bad things can happen. My thermos was open in my sled and it leaked everywhere for sixty miles, so I didn't even have anything available to drink. That was a big part of my learning curve, but not as big as my first Iditarod.

I didn't have any idea what to prepare for because I didn't know what was coming. Everything from packing food drop bags to just knowing what the trail was like and how far it was between certain checkpoints, I had no idea. And I really had no idea how to run the dogs in any kind of logical way as far as a rest-run schedule went. But I muddled through.

I learned so much: how to handle a tired dog team and what sleep deprivation does to me. Every race is like a platform from which you build to the next race.

Although I finished, I actually felt bad when I was done. I felt like I really hadn't performed up to my potential and that the team hadn't performed. I tried to race, but I didn't know how to race.

In Koyuk I took a nineteen-hour break because two dogs sat down and I didn't know what to do about it. I turned around and waited, thinking they would magically snap out of it, which they don't do.

Every time I finish a race, I make a list of everything I've ever done wrong. It's one of my favorite little things I do. I decided to do the Iditarod again. I couldn't think past that first race. But the minute I finished, I thought, I've gotta do this again.

I have made big improvements every year, but you never know. Anything is possible. Your dogs can get sick. Anything can happen, and you have to be ready for it. When I finished twenty-third the next year, I was ecstatic. Once I was preparing for the second one, I really started to think of the Iditarod as something I would do every year.

That became my winter goal. I love being in it. I'm happy when I'm racing. It doesn't have to be the Iditarod, necessarily, but when I'm in a race I really feel good. Physically, I don't always feel good. My feet can be wet or my body can be achy, or I'm tired. I can feel awful. But there's a certain really cool thing about racing. I've heard surfers talk about how they have an almost spiritual experience when they're surfing and everything's working right. I think racing's a little bit like that.

Being out in the winter, being out in the country, that's a huge part of it. I just love my little old, twenty-five-mile training trail behind the house. Parts of it I love seeing every year: the sunset, just being out when the dogs are cooking along. But I also have a competitive streak.

I was a lot happier after my second race. My third year, I was especially racing against myself because I had blown up so much in my first year on the same route. I was getting my second crack at the southern route. I still didn't have a lot of confidence. I still respected the good teams too much.

I was just trying to get the dogs to move at a good speed and have a good run-rest schedule. I think it was around Eagle Island (770 miles into the race) that I realized I was probably going to be in the top twenty, and that was a great feeling. When I came in fifteenth, I was surprised. You just try to run the team the very, very best that you can, and the place sort of takes care of itself.

The next year, I made out a schedule that I thought would put me into the top ten. I only have twenty-five dogs, and I race against mushers who have one hundred dogs in their kennels. And some of mine, maybe eight, are yearlings. Part of the training is to train hard, but also to back off so the dogs don't get hurt. I don't have much of a margin.

I never told people that I could place in the top ten. There was just no way I would say that. But I did have an "A" plan. For many mushers, it's usually to win. Mine was simply to be in the top ten.

The 2002 race was the first year I had a plan that would allow me to finish in 9½ days. That was my goal. I thought that time would put me in the top ten. It was a very simple plan: six hours on, six hours off, almost no matter where I was, whether or not I was at a checkpoint.

Weather conditions didn't get in the way. That could have changed it completely. But everybody would have to deal with the weather. The plan worked well from the restart in Wasilla. I ran the dogs through the heat of the day for six hours straight to Yentna. It took exactly six hours, and I thought that was good.

Other people camped, so I was going without a broken trail. There were a lot of snowmachines and airplanes. The dogs weren't sure where they were going. After four hours, I wanted to take off, but Ramy Brooks talked me into staying another two hours. That's a really good tactic, to tell another competitor to stop. But he was right. He was being honest when he said that it seemed like the best thing to do.

I bit the bullet and stayed. It was just getting to be sunset when I left, so I could run the dogs straight through to Skwentna, camp out not far from Finger Lake for five hours in the middle of the night, run for 5½ hours, and go straight through to Rainy Pass. It was just a very, very predictable schedule, and a lot of people were doing it. It got the dogs in a pattern.

I had started fourth, so a lot of guys behind me were going to make up time on me when their staggered start times were factored into their twenty-four-hour layover. I really didn't have any idea what was going on in the race, but I knew I was running well. I broke a sled going through the Farewell Burn, and I broke a sled runner in Takotna. I had to declare my twenty-four even though I wanted to go on to Cripple. Rick Swenson loaned me a sled to take the rest of the way. It was his starting sled. I had to switch.

The second sled shouldn't have broken. It was an old sled; I shouldn't have had it. But I'm on a budget and it was old, and that's the way it goes. Ken Anderson came up to me and said, "Hey, you're in tenth place." I said, "Yeah, that's pretty good." I knew it didn't mean a whole lot 440 miles into the race, but it felt good.

I was fortunate that Swenson had the sled right there. I still would have had another sled, because Vern Halter had one back at Nikolai that I would have paid a lot of money to fly in. I would have gotten another sled somehow, but I was lucky that Rick had one right there. I could load my stuff quickly, and it didn't cost me any money. And it was a good sled.

I took off from Takotna with this vague idea that if I ran for six hours and rested for six hours, that in three 6-hour runs I could go straight through to Ruby without even stopping in Cripple. I just had to camp on the trail twice. And it worked. It broke down to perfect math. That's where the dogs seemed to start understanding what was going on. It was between zero and twenty degrees at night, but I barely noticed. I didn't look at a thermometer. Even leaving Cripple, where I picked up a bale of straw, the dogs were smoking. That was one of my best runs.

The neat thing about my run-rest schedule was that it coincided with the warm weather and cooler weather. Right around noon I would shut down for six hours, and then I would start back up. It worked almost the whole way. It was in Ruby, on the Yukon River, that I started to think I could have a top-ten finish.

I saw Martin Buser, DeeDee Jonrowe, and John Baker, and I realized that I had to try a little move to get a jump on some people. It took me only four hours or so to reach Nulato. I thought I had another hour or so in the dogs. Instead of stopping, I got a bunch of dog food and some straw, took off out of Nulato, and camped farther down the Yukon toward Kaltag.

Then the wind started. I was in a windstorm. Vern Halter came along while I was booting up, and I pulled the hook. From that point on, we ran together. The windstorm picked up. It was blowing really hard, and when we got to Kaltag they told us we were better off camping down the trail somewhere. I didn't want to stay in Kaltag, anyway, because we had been mushing for only three hours. We kept going until we came to a cabin and had a long campout there. It was around midnight. The dogs got a lot of sleep and a lot of food.

When I got to Unalakleet, where the race comes to the Bering Sea coast and there are fewer than three hundred miles left, I realized what the situation was. I thought, Whoa, wait a minute, I'm in sixth place. Gosh.

I think John Baker was still there, and he was getting ready to leave. DeeDee was there, and she was starting to leave when she saw us show up. Then there were Jeff King and Ramey Smyth behind us, and those are two people you don't want right behind you. Those guys definitely know how to finish a race.

My team took off out of Unalakleet really well, and the dogs basically had to claw their way over glare ice and through wind. I wondered what they were going to do, because it was eight hundred miles into the race. But they did great. They moved straight ahead and we got to Shaktoolik in five hours, almost half an hour faster than any of the front-running teams. That helped me stay ahead of Jeff.

When I got to Shaktoolik, people asked, "Who are you?" And

when I answered, "Jon Little," they said, "Oh, Jon Little," like they knew who I was. That's the first place that ever happened. Before, I was just a guy who had a dog team.

This was also my first exposure to coming into checkpoints that are still fresh, where people have a good attitude and everything is new and they're still having a good time. People in the community hadn't gotten tired of the race yet.

I never had a complaint. The checkpoints were always great, but there was a certain energy at Shaktoolik that I hadn't felt before. At the checkpoint there is basically one room you go into. Vern was sitting there in a chair, and there were probably ten people watching him as he took off his boots and told a story. I'd never seen that kind of attention before. And the doughnuts in Shaktoolik were really good. The other times, they were all gone when I got there.

Shaktoolik to Koyuk has always been a tough run for me. It's just very intimidating psychologically. It's flat. It's open. It fries my dogs. But this year they just marched right through. It wasn't really fast, but we had no problems. That's also when we really started racing. We started taking five-hour breaks, a little less rest.

The dogs were still barking, lively. My team got up off the straw trotting and barking; that's a discouragement factor for other mushers. Martin Buser and Ramy Brooks were out of sight, and I didn't know where John Baker was. But Vern and I started talking about how maybe we could catch DeeDee. We weren't planning to run together. But I would leave a checkpoint first and he would catch me, or he would leave first and I would catch him.

People picked up on the fact that Vern and I were neck-and-neck. They thought perhaps there was some cutthroat race going on between us, but there wasn't. There was definitely more media coverage than I'd ever seen before.

We only took a two-hour rest at Elim. I didn't like doing it, but it was the right thing to do in the race. It wasn't enough; the dogs were a little stiff leaving. But I knew the next rest was going to be the eight-hour layover in White Mountain. The dogs were still going well, and then they really started speeding up again. I realized that even going up the hill that we call Little McKinley, the team was going at speeds I was used to going in training runs. I was just euphoric.

Vern was going at the same speed, and then we saw a light up ahead. At first it seemed it might be one of the many snowmachines around. I said, "I think that's DeeDee." And it was.

We passed by. It was about ten or fifteen miles short of Golovin. It was an area that's just a big, flat expanse with nothing but trail markers in a straight line into the town. Vern went by DeeDee first, but then I passed him. Leaving Golovin, I was in fourth place, but Vern passed me back heading into White Mountain three minutes ahead.

In White Mountain I had eight hours to think about things. One of my favorite things was looking at the chalkboard and seeing that Ramey Smyth and Jeff King were 2 or 2½ hours behind me. I thought, That's comfortable enough. Short of something really horrible happening, I'm gonna come in fifth. That was an amazing feeling. That was just awesome.

I knew I could feel good about the race no matter what. That's where I decided I wasn't going to race Vern. But Andy Anderson, one of the race marshals, came up to me and put his hand on my shoulder. He said, "You know, something could happen next year. You could fall off a barstool. You may never be in this position again. Enjoy it." I thought that was good advice.

Somewhere along the way to the blowhole after we left the Top-kok Hills, I started thinking, "Wait a minute. I really may never be in this position again. I have a shot to compete for fourth place in the Iditarod. Why would I just sit back and coast in? That's crazy."

I started calling the dogs up for more speed. The other reason was that it was starting to get hot. We were in the blowhole area, but there was no wind. The place can turn into a desert. It can just feel barren and the dogs can suffer. I got them into Safety, the last checkpoint, as quickly as I could. And I could see a little black dot up ahead of me. It was Vern and his team.

Vern had a leader that was starting to have a problem. Right then my team started to run a little faster. We passed Vern and I said, "Let's make it a race." There were about ten or eleven miles left. Knowing he was right behind me, I kept telling the dogs to go faster. I whistled and ski-poled and ran as hard as I could past Cape Nome, which was hard. I was gasping and stumbling.

The dogs started acting a little tired, and I realized I had better shut up and let them run their own race. In fact, I stopped and snacked them. Vern was a dot on the horizon behind me. The dogs cruised at a nice, steady pace the last five miles to Front Street.

It was about six o'clock at night, right around sunset. I had the luxury of my team loping to the finish line. The siren announcing my arrival went off really late, so essentially there was no warning that I was coming. There weren't many people watching.

But I was standing under the arch on Front Street, in fourth place in the Iditarod, with a time of 9 days, 7 hours, 22 minutes. It felt awesome. I think I told someone there that it hadn't sunk in yet. It really hadn't, either. I think it took weeks for it to sink in.

As far as I was concerned, I'd just had a really good race. The team was just doing what I expected it to do, and finishing that high was really cool, but I didn't realize that's pretty hard to do. It really settled in later. It's definitely a feather in your cap. Nobody can ever take that away from you. You have accomplished that. It is hard to do, and few people do it. And it was the ninth fastest time in the race's history. I was twenty-five minutes ahead of Vern. He says he stopped to have a beer somewhere.

Knowing that I had one of the top ten fastest finishes ever is just a great feeling. We could not have done any better. There were hardly any decisions I could have made better.

Sometimes I say it out loud, that I have one of the ten fastest times. It still surprises me, especially considering where I came from. The first few races I ran, I was way back in the pack. I got one red lantern (in a shorter race). Everything came together. The dogs were strong, and I had a great time.

RACE RECORD

1992	14 days, 4 hours, 12 minutes	43rd
1994	11 days, 1 hour, 38 minutes	7th
1995	9 days, 14 hours, 58 minutes	5th
1996	9 days, 22 hours	7th
1997	9 days, 23 hours, 49 minutes	13th
1998	9 days, 11 hours, 41 minutes	3rd
1999	10 days, 9 hours, 19 minutes	5th
2000	9 days, 11 hours, 16 minutes	5th
2001	12 days, 2 hours, 26 minutes	20th
2002	9 days, 13 hours, 36 minutes	8th
2003	Scratched	

CHAPTER 21

CHARLIE BOULDING

H e talks with a North Carolina drawl, his trademark
white hair hangs in long braids, and in some ways
the white-bearded Charlie Boulding, sixty, who lives on a
rural homestead near Manley, resembles singer Willie Nelson.
Boulding, who lives deep in the Alaska Bush, off the road system,
with his wife, Robin, is considered the oldest serious Iditarod-
title contender.

Boulding took up mushing in Montana to help his trapping,
buying dogs from a guy moving to Saudi Arabia. He read a how-
to book, but he still needed a neighbor's suggestion that he use
neck lines to better hold the dogs. He moved to Alaska in 1983,
after more than two years of sobriety following an earlier life
plagued with alcohol problems. He said he hasn't had a drink
or a haircut since.

Soon after he established residency, Boulding met wife Robin
hitchhiking with six dogs on the Dalton Highway in the Brooks
Range, though they didn't get together for good until later. He
also claimed a five-acre parcel of land thirty miles upriver from
Manley. The closest neighbor is five miles away, and Boulding
lived in a tent for six years, struggling to make a living.

Boulding started mushing, won the Yukon Quest twice, and
shifted to the Iditarod in 1992. In November 2002, when Boulding
and Robin spoke about his life in mushing, he was battling colon
cancer and had just come from a Fairbanks hospital where he
had a chemotherapy treatment.

One day, my trapping partner and I were setting in the cabin in camp and I had some mail. I'd broken my glasses, and I said, "Who's this from?" He said it was from "a Robin." I said, "Oh, that girl. What does it say?" He said I'd best be looking for a job and a place to stay next year. I said, "Why?" He said she wanted to become my handler.

We were together for four years before we got married. Robin popped the question, actually. We were at the Toledo Polo Club for the wedding of a member of her family, and it was time for the family picture. In her family, the rule was that you couldn't be in the picture unless you were married. We hadn't talked much about getting married. She came up to me and said, "Are you going to marry me or not?" I said, "Do I have to tell you right this minute?" I was surrounded by all of her relatives. She said, "Yes!" She had to know whether or not I was going to be in the picture. She got me cornered there.

I did the Quest in 1989 and finished tenth, but I got penalized and knocked back to eleventh. I won in 1991 and in 1993. Robin was supposed to stay over for one winter, but she decided she was interested in fishing, too.

The way I finished in 1990, going 250 miles in forty-eight hours, showed me the dogs were tough. When I finished, I was lying there, about dead. I could hardly move. Robin came over and I said, "I can win this damn thing." She laughed and said, "You look like it."

The next year, I was head-to-head with Bruce Lee, but I had this hole card. I had a dog team that, if need be, could go for forty out of forty-eight hours. The people I'd talked to thought I was lying or crazy, or they didn't believe it.

I held back until I got to Valley Center. That's forty miles out of Fairbanks. I thought it was a little far out, but if I couldn't hold him off I'd pass him on the Chena River. I passed him at Valley Center and he never caught me. They clocked us on the last measured mile at fifteen miles an hour.

Everybody was cheering. It was in the morning and the military, the offices, let everyone out. It was on the radio, a live broadcast. Hundreds of people were lined up on the Chena River.

In 1992 I ran the Quest and the Iditarod. I finished forty-third in the Iditarod. But I took all of the dogs I normally would have gotten rid of that year and put them in one team. The next year, 1994, I finished seventh.

I took the dogs on really long runs. People like Rick Swenson and Susan Butcher were still running traditional Alaskan huskies, bigger dogs, and Iditarod mushers weren't taking such long runs. I knew those guys weren't dumb; they would start doing what we were doing. I just stumbled on my training techniques. We weren't influenced by the established long-distance mushers because we didn't know anybody. I figured we had about two years to capitalize.

I'm a nuts-and-bolts guy. If it works, do it. If it doesn't work, the hell with it; do something else. I had a training regimen that was very different at the time for length of mileage on runs and the speed that I trained at.

I felt sort of inefficient, though, because most of the guys I was running with had seven, eight, ten Iditarods under their belts, and I was making rookie mistakes with a really nice dog team. I'd look at my dogs and I'd look at their dogs, and I'd think, "Hey, I've got as good dogs as anybody, but I'm making fool mistakes." I did that for the first three years. By the time I stopped making mistakes and got the race figured out, everybody was caught up.

It was satisfying to come in seventh. I never have kept my cards close to my chest. I'm not a poker player. When I found out something worked and somebody asked me, "How do you do this?" I'd tell them, Well, I train this way, or I feed that way, or I do this, or I do that. I love the sport, and I think the sport progresses by people sharing their knowledge. A lot of the young guys who came to me and asked questions are beating me now.

There isn't any secret ingredient. People thought I was crazy because I'd send out beef and lamb and nothing else, just commercial meat. Everybody was sending out nine different kinds of this and that. I said that if you run the dogs hard enough and they burn up energy, they've got to replenish it. The theory then was that if you ran them too hard, they wouldn't eat. I thought that didn't add up.

If you burn calories, you have to replenish them.

The 1998 race, when I finished third, was probably my most regrettable, disappointing, and memorable. It was my best finish, but that's not what made it the most memorable.

I was in transition. I was rebuilding my team. I had won the Kuskokwim 300 the year before with seven- and eight-year-old dogs. Everybody was asking, "How the hell do you win a fast race with old dogs?" I said, "You've got to have old, good dogs." But all of my old guys couldn't make the speed anymore. I finished thirteenth in the Iditarod in 1997.

I was going from my older dogs to a whole new bunch. It was a young team, but it had a lot of talent. I was pretty happy with them. I did the Copper Basin and the Kuskokwim 300 with these young dogs, and in both places they sort of petered out at the end. I made money, but they didn't perform the way I was used to seeing my old dogs perform. I went into the 1998 Iditarod with a nice little dog team and a very young leader that I didn't have much confidence in.

We started the race pretty far back in the order, but the dogs were moving well. I got to the Yukon River and they were moving even better. I was in the top fifteen.

That was the year they put the checkpoint for Galena on the Yukon River. I was sort of teed off. It was open to the wind, out there with no protection. I got there and said, "To hell with this." I could camp just as well anywhere on the Yukon, so I didn't want to bother staying there. I threw some food and straw in my sled and took off.

Everybody else was still in Galena. Nobody goes straight through Galena. But I know the river, and I went down to Bishop Mountain, a big landmark. I'd gone from fifteenth to second. DeeDee Jonrowe was way ahead, but everyone else was pretty much grouped together. Jeff King came in and asked, "Where's Charlie?" They told him I had left. He ran around, ripped open his supply bag, got some food and straw, and he left, too, chasing me.

At Bishop Mountain I set up a camp. I reckon I'd been camped there for about half an hour, and here came Jeff. He went across the river from me and mushed out of sight. I didn't know until the next morning when I went that he had camped only about two hundred yards farther down the river. That move catapulted us ahead. We mushed out of there and went straight to Kaltag. We didn't stop in Galena. We didn't stop in Nulato.

DeeDee was still way ahead. The move I made, with Jeff following, was a big move. Rick Swenson and Vern Halter and all of those guys stopped in Nulato. I had always wanted to make that move, but the impetus at the time was that I was ticked off.

DeeDee and Jeff were ahead of me out of Kaltag. It was a three-team race until I made a mistake on the way to Unalakleet. I stopped at Old Woman cabin. I thought Jeff was there. I misread the equipment I saw on the scene. It actually belonged to some local dogsledder who wasn't in the race. I went on by and camped off to the side, figuring I was being cagey.

But they both had already gone through. I took a fairly long break waiting for DeeDee and Jeff to show up, and they never showed. That was a mistake. That cost me critical time. That got me out of sight of them, which was bad. Jeff was getting short on dogs, so I was really disappointed because we were really running well.

I never put the push on them. That was my fault. I didn't ask the dogs for more because they were young and I had a young leader. I didn't really trust them. It would have been easier to do if second place had been in sight. I've always been someone who didn't let other mushers dictate my race. I race my own race. I've always done it. But in that circumstance I would have been better off running their race. Sometimes you need to chase.

I had time left. I had the team. In retrospect, I had the team that could have done it. Jeff came in first, about three hours ahead of DeeDee, and she was about three hours ahead of me. A friend of mine, Freddy Jordan, was there when they came in. He thought their teams were just about shot. Then I came in, and I was just screaming down Front Street.

My team came in happy, jumping around, wouldn't even lie down. I was so disappointed that I didn't have the confidence to make that push. It was obvious to me at the end that I could have made a push anywhere between Unalakleet and White Mountain and made up that little time I had lost at Old Woman. I could have actually capitalized on that because I had rested and they hadn't. I had a fresher team. It was musher error that I came in third. I came in third with what I felt was a first-place team.

It was regrettable that I didn't read the dogs well enough to make that push. It was memorable because it was a hell of a nice dog team. It was probably the most talented team I'd ever had up until my team for the 2003 race. They were more talented than my old guys that were so dependable. Evidently, I didn't know how to capitalize on that talent.

I didn't wish I was first, I knew I should have been first. That's sort of hard to take, when you think the dogs were there and I had trained them right. I'm noted for gutsy mushing.

I was just being conservative. I'm usually anything but conservative. And the money came into play. I got to thinking that if I pushed those young guys and something happened, I wouldn't be in third place, I might end up in tenth place. That's the difference between making almost $39,000 and making only $19,000 or so.

All of those numbers were going through my head. The numbers felt very real, and the money caused me to back off. Well, not back off, but not push hard. I was disappointed in myself.

When I started racing dogs, I was just a trapper with a dog team who lived in the Bush. Now, people recognize me on the streets in Alaska. That's pretty surprising. But this is very much a "we" operation. Robin is the catalyst. If it weren't for her, none of this would have happened except for maybe my first race in the Quest. I don't know if I would still be doing it if it weren't for Robin. She loves it. I think she loves it more than I do.

Of course, I'd like to win. I may have started off out of the Bush doing things differently from other people, but I like to kick butt. I like to be on top. I'm not a high ego person, but I am a high achiever. I want to win. I don't think I have an overinflated ego, but everybody has some.

I'll stick with the Iditarod as long as it's comfortable. I do have bad knees. The left one is particularly bad. The cartilage is shot. There's no cartilage, it's bone on bone. I've had surgery on it. My knees slow me down on the trail.

I discovered the colon cancer in June of 2002. I didn't really feel bad or anything, but I noticed a change in the stool. From my reading, I knew that was a symptom of colon problems. I went in for a colonoscopy, and there it was. It was June 16, and I had an operation a week later. My energy level is not what it was, from the chemotherapy.

I'm anemic. The chemo's keeping my red-cell count down.

Luckily, contrary to what most people experience, my white-cell count has stayed good and high. It didn't stop me from training or planning to be in the Iditarod again. I've got the best bunch of dogs I've ever had.

RACE RECORD

1992	11 days, 13 hours, 47 minutes	9th
1993	11 days, 6 hours, 38 minutes	8th
1994	11 days	6th
1995	9 days, 2 hours, 42 minutes	1st
1996	9 days, 8 hours, 32 minutes	2nd
1997	9 days, 11 hours, 41 minutes	2nd
1998	9 days, 22 hours, 34 minutes	9th
1999	9 days, 14 hours, 3 minutes	1st
2000	9 days, 58 minutes	1st
2001	9 days, 19 hours, 55 minutes	1st
2002	13 days, 5 hours, 24 minutes	40th

CHAPTER 22

DOUG SWINGLEY

Lincoln, Montana, musher Doug Swingley, fifty, holds many distinctions in the Iditarod Trail Sled Dog Race. Swingley was rookie of the year in 1992, became the first musher from outside of Alaska to win the championship in 1995, and is one of four competitors to win the title four times. He and Susan Butcher are the only mushers to win three Iditarod championships in succession. Swingley is also the oldest musher to win the Iditarod.

Swingley owns ten top-10 finishes and twice set race speed records between Anchorage and Nome. The former mink rancher broke into the sport with his brother Greg as a partner, but now operates his kennel with wife Melanie Shirilla, whom he married on Front Street in Nome in 2002.

During that 2002 Iditarod, Swingley entered the race as the favorite to become the first musher to win four straight titles, but soon after it began, he slowed his team and chose to make his run to Nome a non-competitive tourist trip. He said he plans to return to the race and also try the Yukon Quest.

Along with Martin Buser and Jeff King, the sometimes blunt-spoken Swingley traded Iditarod championships for eleven races in a row. During the 2003 race, Swingley flew his new airplane from Montana to Alaska and was a television commentator on the trail.

I was always good at any sport I tried—baseball, wrestling, and football—when I was growing up. I always wanted to win, and I wouldn't participate if I didn't think I had the opportunity to win. From the very first sled dog race I was involved with as a handler for my brother Greg in 1989, I looked at the possibility of making it a career. I think a huge percentage of Iditarod mushers just want to get to the finish line. I want to win.

I've enjoyed the lifestyle of working with dogs immensely. You always have dreams of putting it together and making a career out of it, but I don't think you can ever anticipate what it's going to be like when you get there. Ranching was my career before dog mushing, and it was not a huge change in my lifestyle.

My first Iditarod, in 1992, I learned a whole bunch. I started racing in 1989, so I had some time to be what I considered seasoned by my first Iditarod. I was too naive to realize you are not seasoned until you've done it. The Iditarod was just another dog race to me, so I felt I could win or, if nothing else, be competitive. I finished ninth, and I was unhappy with my performance.

I'm the ultimate competitor, and I'm only happy with perfection, which people now know defines my career. I think I let everybody know after the race was over how I felt, and maybe that's where I got the "cocky" prefix to my name. I think a lot of people would have been gushing about how well they had done.

In the past, even mushers who entered the Iditarod from other states moved to Alaska if they did well, but I think people have realized that I am a fourth generation Montanan and I'm not going to move to Alaska. I haven't changed who I am. Everybody else who has ever been a competitor moved to Alaska, because it is more difficult if you don't live there.

There are logistical problems, living in Montana. I've overcome what a lot of people thought was not possible. I found a training area and a great place to develop a dog team for the Iditarod, and I don't think anybody can argue with that now. There's still the logistical problem of getting the dogs to Alaska.

My race starts long before someone in Alaska starts, because I have to drive twenty-four hundred miles up the highway to get my

dogs there. I have to get there early because I can't have the vet check them anywhere but there. The Iditarod makes it a lot easier for an Alaskan to get ready for the Iditarod than it does for a Montanan, or a European, or anyone else. They make the same demands on us that they would make if we lived in downtown Anchorage.

When I won in 1995, everyone assumed it was just a fluke, even though I set a new record of 9 days, 2 hours, 42 minutes. There was a feeling that everyone else failed and I succeeded. Then, when I took second the next two years, it was a major defeat. A lot of people would be tickled to death to take second place, but because it was me, I was laughed at because I didn't win. That was largely because I was from outside of Alaska. The people of Alaska wanted their trophy back. And every time I got beat, Alaskans felt vindicated as the best mushers.

By 2000, when I had won the race three times and it was apparent that I wasn't going anywhere, there seemed to be thoughts that maybe there's a secret weapon. Maybe the altitude where I trained being more than a mile high. But by 2000 I was secure that this wasn't a fluke, and I just laughed about it.

I didn't think I was doing anything different from anybody else in Alaska. I was just working hard, and I came up with a phenomenal group of dogs and understood them, and understood the race. There were no secrets.

I think that any time you don't go someone else's way, people would rather think that you had some advantage than think they didn't do something right. A lot of Alaskans, and certainly my competitors, wanted to believe that I had some advantage. They certainly didn't want to point fingers at one of their mushers for not doing something right.

No one is unbeatable. There's a bank of information that I use. It all comes down to implementing all of this information into a plan and making it so... not that you're unbeatable... but so you have an opportunity to win.

I think it's distracting to think that way, that someone is unbeatable. I think it's more distracting to the individual. In this sport, hope springs eternal. Alaskans didn't care which Alaskan won, they just hoped an Alaskan would win. It became more distracting to me because now I had everybody against me.

Dog mushing is not an individual sport. We're dealing with a whole bunch of volunteers, sixteen of them, that we're telling what to do, and they depend on us 100 percent. The difference between human sports and dog sports is that the musher is also the manager. He can have the biggest ego in the world, he can build his plan off all of these slights, and build a vendetta against whomever he wants to battle, but it won't do any good if he can't implement it with his teammates.

Probably my most fun Iditarod was when I won in 1995, my fourth race. I had been sixth the year before, so I was definitely a top-ten guy, but I was not seen as a top contender. I had run enough races to know I was going to be in the top ten, but I don't think when it started that I was convinced I was going to win. At some point in your career, you have the ability to identify a great dog team, but this was my first observation of everything coming together. It was the most fun because I knew the dogs were having as much fun as I was, and that there were all kinds of possibilities.

By the time I got to Unalakleet, I knew it was going to be very difficult for anyone to keep up with me. That made it gratifying. But it was agonizing to know that I had to keep going for 2½ more days before I found out. It's like being a kid before Christmas. You know that the presents are all under the tree, but you won't get to open them for a few days.

I'm never really super-exuberant in Nome, because I've kind of emotionally gone through the whole thing in my mind the last few miles. I think the happiness and joy come between Safety and into Nome. You know you're going to get there, the last twenty-two miles. That's when mounds of emotion overcome you, especially the first time. I'm obviously happy that I've won, but I'm not jumping up and down like a little kid. I'm emotionally exhausted because of the last twenty miles.

The victory meant that I had solidified my career as a dog

musher, and now it was going to be a lifestyle. At least in the mid-1990s, it meant a career financially. I never really felt that I was representing other mushers who came from outside of Alaska. I've never felt that I was any different from any of my competitors; I just came from a different place.

I think what I realized after that—and what the Iditarod found out—is that my win enlightened more of the world about the Iditarod. All of a sudden this guy from Outside went up there and won an Alaska event. Whether or not Alaska wanted to admit it, it was still perceived as an Alaska event until I won it, and then that brought more of the world into it.

I just happened to be the first guy from Outside, the way Libby Riddles was the first woman. All of a sudden, all kinds of doors opened for women to race in the Iditarod. They thought, Well, if Libby can win, so can I. It gave them hope, and it brought a whole lot of fans in from all over. When I won, fans of a musher from Michigan no longer had to look at him as just a guy who was going to Alaska to run the Iditarod. They could look at him as a guy who could go up there and win. I realized that after I won, but honestly, I didn't care about that right away. It took me time to realize it.

By the time I got home to Montana, my answering machine was filled with messages from people who wanted me to go places. I think I traveled 250,000 air miles in 1995. It was a bit overwhelming. You don't sign up for the Iditarod anticipating that kind of reception when you win. You're winning for your own ego and for your own values. All of a sudden you start picking up the phone and people from all over the world are asking you to do things.

The level of interest was worldwide. Then it sunk in that I was the first from Outside to do that. It was agonizing when I didn't win again right away. Remember, I was the guy from Outside. I was a very confident individual, and I couldn't do it again. It was so easy in 1995, and all of a sudden it became difficult. I had the obligations of being a professional musher, making appearances, and representing companies, and some of it was misery. I was relieved when I won in 1999. I don't think I was as excited or happy as I was relieved.

With every race you win, you step closer to infamy. Maybe it's lasting fame, but it becomes infamy because it's hard to find people who have positive things to say about people who win too much. When Susan Butcher won three in a row in 1986, 1987, and 1988, people didn't care who beat her, they just wanted someone else to win.

I think Alaskans finally accepted me after I won in 2000 and in 2001. It was sustained excellence, and the fact that I was able to withstand the stoning. They had thrown all of the negatives at me, and I could still do just as well as I had always done. That bred admiration: "He just must be good."

My hardest victory occurred in the 2001 race. The 2000 race was hard because I fractured two ribs. I was on massive amounts of Aleve. It happened in the first mile between Wasilla and Knik, so I went a long ways with it.

But that was a phenomenal dog team, where I could have hung on to win even if I had been a paraplegic. I think, though, at that point there were people who finally realized that I was the real thing. If you can make something like an injury useful, that is. And I broke two sleds that year. Some people appreciate indications that you might be tough. But the conditions were fairly easy. I wouldn't have wanted broken ribs in 2001.

Because 2001 was the toughest race in my career, it was the most satisfying. It was Mother Nature's vendetta against dog mushers. There was no snow at the start of the race. We had to change the location of the start to Willow. The conditions for the first few hundred miles were satisfactory, and the temperature was OK. It didn't get over thirty degrees during the day. The conditions weren't as bad as we anticipated, so we got lulled into this false sense of security. When we left Rohn, all hell broke loose.

I blasted through Rohn, but I picked up a few followers. Everybody had caught on to Doug Swingley's plan. Paul Gebhardt, Mitch Seavey, Rick Swenson, Rick Mackey, Jerry Riley, and DeeDee Jonrowe followed. I was not lonely. Now there was no snow and the trail was very rough. The frozen tussocks and sticks and stumps made it very dangerous. Mushers think mainly of survival on a trail like that.

We had to be on our toes. The race didn't mean a thing. Now we were running on bare ground. We were running in little dust clouds. It was hard to see because of dirt flying. Instead of a blizzard, it was dirt. We were dodging stumps and sticks and rocks, and the foremost thing on our minds was just getting to Nikolai. There were a lot of wrecks in there. I was fortunate. I was 100 percent healthy. The team got through it without too many malfunctions.

Nothing broke that I couldn't fix, and in Nikolai I kind of re-grouped and felt I had dodged a bullet. Now the race was back on. We fixed our bruises. I was black and blue. The trail was as bad as anybody had seen it. I think DeeDee launched over her sled a couple of times. We found broken pieces of equipment on the trail.

It was better leaving Nikolai, and I've always felt the test of the caliber of my dog team is between Nikolai and McGrath. I know that trail is always going to be good. If I had done any damage to the dog team in those tough circumstances, it was going to show up. I let the dogs stretch out a little bit to see if we had created any problems, and the team was just perfect. Cola, Abby, Peppy, and Stormy were the main leaders.

Everything was going according to plan. The team fired like it was supposed to, and when we reached Takotna I was confident that I had most of the competition in hand. I stayed six hours, then took off for what I thought was going to be a fairly uneventful run to Iditarod and cruised through Ophir. All of a sudden, about twenty miles outside of Ophir, there was no snow again. To me, this is a worse place to be without snow. I found out it definitely was worse going than between Rohn and Nikolai. The country is hilly and filled with tussocks. There was no trail.

The salvation between Rohn and Nikolai was that the dogs had something to follow, even if it was an indentation in the tundra where it had been packed down and we were just following a dirt furrow. But between Ophir and Iditarod, there was none of that because the trail is not used by anyone. If you go to Iditarod, you use an airplane. Even the trail setters couldn't find the trail. At one point I was within two hundred yards of where I'd already been after going five miles. That was extra mileage I hadn't planned on traveling. It was very, very rough.

It was almost impossible for the dogs to pull with me standing on the runners, and I think I had fourteen dogs at that point. The tundra tussocks were like going across sandpaper. I trudged on foot behind, running when I could, and the dogs slowed to a virtual walk. Even when we hit downhill parts, they refused to speed up because the footing was so insecure.

This was the first time in my career that I had seen the dogs in self-survival mode. There was an inch of snow here and there. Peppy, who has never been long on brains, realized that if he followed the snowmachine tracks, we'd be on the trail. He learned it on his own. I got to Iditarod first, without too much damage to the dog team. I was happy about that.

You know it is going to be just as tough for the other mushers, so you think that if somebody else gets through it better than you did, you just have to accept it and wait for the next challenge. And this was going to be a year of challenges. I could see that already, so it wasn't as if I should be depressed if I couldn't go as fast as the next guy, because maybe the next challenge I would do better.

Linwood Fiedler decided to go on to Anvik, and it was thrilling for everyone to see that someone was going to be innovative. I knew I had a better dog team, though. The terrain to Shageluk wasn't a whole lot better than getting into Iditarod. At Grayling I was going into a ground blizzard on the Yukon River. There was no relief, no trees, no protection from Mother Nature. The wind was thirty miles an hour right into my face. Visibility was nil. It was getting dark, and I knew visibility was going to be even more impaired by the blowing snow. For five or ten miles I kept thinking, Maybe I should go back.

I never thought of turning around on the Iditarod Trail before. I always had the utmost confidence in that dog team that if I pointed them in one direction, they were prepared to go to it. But I was starting to believe that maybe this was a strategic mistake. I figured I had gotten myself into this thing, and now I had to find the best way out of it.

It was cold. It was windy. The wind chill was probably minus-twenty or minus-thirty. The snow was blowing badly, and the trail was soft. I had trouble choosing leaders that would complement each other. I won't tell you that I wasn't cold out there, but I wasn't worried about dying or not surviving. I was more concerned about my dog team.

I ended up with Peppy and Vuarnet—like the sunglasses—in lead, and it worked out great. Only by that circumstance did I find an incredible leader, and I made it through to Eagle Island. I liken it to a training run. You don't ask the dogs to do anything but work cohesively until you get to the next spot. You're just getting to the next point. I stopped whenever the wind was blowing and petted them and fed them several times.

There were some bad sections of trail and windy sections, and I was happy to get to Kaltag. After 150 miles on the Yukon River, I was happy to get off it. Once again, the dogs were vibrant and willing to eat, which reaffirmed the fact that I was easy on them.

We were on the Bering Sea coast now, and we were at the mercy of the wind. There were some difficult times. It was the only time I had to walk in front of my dogs, between Elim and White Mountain. At the top of Little McKinley the wind was howling, there was fresh snow, and visibility was down to less than twenty feet. I at least had the solace that with every step, I was one step closer to Nome. We went through a herd of caribou, and that was spectacular.

After White Mountain, when I had seventy or eighty miles to go and an eight-hour lead, everything became calm. I turned on my radio and listened to the KNOM race reports. I heard that my sister, Marvel Lumley, had come in to Nome to greet me. That was a surprise.

It was my hardest and most gratifying race. I think anybody who enters the Iditarod is in it for the adventure. There are a lot of things you can do in your lifetime, but few things will throw as much adventure at you as the Iditarod with sixteen dogs. There are so many variables. I think this was the most adventurous race.

The 2002 race was different. It took restraint for me not to be competitive in 2002. I was proud of myself that I could hold back. I pulled over early and took a rest, and then just took the team to Nome without racing. In all the years I raced the Iditarod, I never had an opportunity to just enjoy it. The Iditarod had always been nine or ten days of the same kind of work I do all year long.

I enjoyed the ability to see the trail at my own pace, largely in daylight. It was fun to see people in the villages whom I hadn't had time to see because my race plan had been to camp on the trail. I had a great time. Always in a competitive Iditarod, I sacrifice certain things. This was the reverse. I had time to stop and do whatever I wanted. I could rest the dogs and I could sleep. I could stay in a village for eight hours instead of four. I had fourteen dogs lope into Nome the way they loped out of Anchorage. I stopped every hour to pet that dog team. I had a great reception of well-wishers.

I proposed to Melanie near Knik, and I surprised her. The

night before the start of the Iditarod, I didn't sleep, which is fairly common. I decided if this gal was willing to put up with my whims and with my decision to do something this crazy and stupid, maybe she'd be willing to accept anything I do from here on out. I wasn't sure she would say yes. I gave her two seconds to think about it just before the Knik Bar—she knew I'd never leave Knik if she didn't answer me. Obviously, she said yes.

I committed to stopping at every checkpoint, and I think I had a drink at every one except Knik. Typically, in Safety, people throw their bibs on and off they go to Nome. But I walked into the bar and said, "Bartender, give me a shot of whiskey." It's like an Old West bar: small, not a lot of room in there. The bartender turned around, saw it was me, and was surprised. He said, "It's on the house."

Some people think I retired from the Iditarod, but I thought I made it clear it was just a sabbatical. I'll be back. Me, and Arnold Schwarzenegger. But I think I want to go and do different things. People don't realize that the Iditarod consumes your life. I will be back, and I will win the Iditarod again at some point. I just don't know when. Maybe sooner than you think.

RACE RECORD

1994	11 days, 15 hours, 41 minutes	17th
1995	10 days, 14 hours, 8 minutes	16th
1996	10 days, 2 hours, 56 minutes	11th
1997	9 days, 21 hours, 51 minutes	8th
1998	10 days, 14 hours, 9 minutes	18th
2000	9 days, 9 hours, 20 minutes	4th
2001	11 days, 20 hours, 47 minutes	12th
2002	9 days, 49 minutes	2nd
2003	9 days, 17 hours, 37 minutes	2nd

CHAPTER 23
RAMY BROOKS

Dog mushing is in the genes of Ramy Brooks, thirty-five, of Healy, Alaska. Brooks has followed the successes of his grandfather Gareth Wright, and his mother, Roxy Wright, with his own elite performances in the Yukon Quest and Iditarod.

Gareth and Roxy Wright both won North American and world sprint championships. Ramy Brooks has excelled at long-distance mushing, and his title-winning effort in the Quest made for three generations of champions in the same family.

Brooks, who is married and has two daughters with wife Cathy, has developed a large following, both because of his excellence on the trail and his Native heritage. He has campaigned against the influences of drugs and alcohol, and urges youngsters to stay in school.

Brooks won Iditarod rookie-of-the-year honors in 1994 and won the Yukon Quest championship in 1999.

Igrew up around dogs, and that had a big part in my dream of wanting to be a mushing champion and winning the Iditarod. I was living in a fish camp in Rampart, and my friends and I used to pretend we had hundred-dog kennels and that we were going to win the Open North American and the Fur Rendezvous World Championship. The first time I dreamed of winning the Iditarod was 1983, when my mom ran the race.

She was training in Rampart until around Christmas, and then we moved by dog team to Eureka. We stayed at Rick Swenson's place and my mom trained there. I got to ride in one of Rick's sleds, and I thought it would be cool to be a four-time champion of the Iditarod like he was.

When I was a teenager, we moved into Fairbanks, and I got to a point where I didn't want to have anything to do with stupid dog chores. They were so much work, and the other kids were doing other things. Taking care of dogs, cleaning up after dogs, I couldn't spend time talking to the other kids. I felt out of place.

I moved to the Lower 48 at the end of high school and was in the Navy. Landlocked, actually, most of the time. I was in California, Colorado, Idaho Falls, and Florida, then Washington for six years. Eventually I realized the big cities were not for me and realized how much I missed the dogs. Growing up in a rural area where there's not a whole lot, you see things on TV and think, "Oh, that would be cool." But when you actually live there and come from a background like mine, you don't enjoy it at all.

When I came back and got into racing, my whole goal became winning the Iditarod. The whole family is extremely competitive, whether we're playing a board game or running a dog team. I'm probably one of the more competitive ones.

It's hard to say whether I'm more competitive than my mom or my grandpa. I think I'm at the top, but when they were in the prime of racing, they might have been. I've seen the intensity, more with my mom than with Grandpa, but I guarantee I'm very focused. When I decided to race, I think they were very happy and excited. I think Grandpa wanted to see somebody using dogs with his bloodlines, the Aurora Husky.

My grandpa had a lot to do with helping me get started and on my own way. I think of Iditarod racing as a long-term commitment. Both Doug Swingley and Rick Swenson won it fairly fast in their careers. Other people have taken quite a few years before working their way to the top. The level of competition has increased over the last ten years. It takes time to get to the top of the field.

When I started in 1994, I was a little impatient. What I learn every year helps me to be more competitive with the field the next year. It's learning little bits of how mentally to deal with the challenges. Every year you find new challenges thrown at you. Dealing with family losses going into a race, dealing with dogs getting sick, dealing with different types of conditions out there. You're never going to face it all in one year. It's about learning to take the punches and being able to keep on going without affecting your race.

I really believe there is a process of learning. In some of my earlier races, not just in the Iditarod, I felt some frustration: Just how do I beat guys like Jeff King and Martin Buser and Doug Swingley and DeeDee Jonrowe? I knew I had a fast team, but what were they doing to end up in front of me? Once, sitting in Shaktoolik, Jeff said, "What do you mean, being frustrated about where you're at? Look at how far you've come in a short time."

When you're trying to reach their level of expertise, I think you're looking at never being able to beat them. You feel like you're taking a step forward and a couple of steps backward, sometimes.

I always go into a race trying to win it, whether that's realistic or not, whether the circumstances are there or not. I guess my rookie year I knew I had a lot to learn. I still didn't really know exactly how to train the dogs, and I was still trying to figure out strategies of where to run and rest, and I didn't know the trail or about checkpoint efficiency.

Checkpoint efficiency is huge. It played a huge factor in my first couple of years. It took me forty-five minutes to an hour to bootie a dog team, and I realized that was a weakness. Even today, when I'm practicing or training, I put myself on a stopwatch putting booties on. Now it takes me 12½ minutes. That's a half-hour of sleep a day. Then there are other chores: putting straw down, snacking the dogs, making a warm meal, going through vet care. You can get much faster at all of those. I can be done with everything in forty-five minutes now. Before, it probably took two or three hours. The dogs get better-quality rest. And I get some rest.

My first year, I stayed with the leaders to Cripple and watched how they did their chores. I probably would have done better that year if I hadn't spent so much time watching them and had gotten some sleep. Then, in Cripple, I overslept by a couple of hours, and I got panicky and didn't run the best second half of the race.

I was in the top twenty for my first five Iditarods, and then I went over to the Quest in 1999 and won it. That was a confidence booster. I think that was a big lesson in learning how to win. When I came back to the Iditarod the next year, I was fourth. I was trying to overcome being sick on the trail and making some bad decisions, but finishing fourth anyway told me I could win it.

I was right there, and I just needed to make a few adjustments and I could do it. And then the next year I came back and things didn't go right from the start. No matter what your goals and intentions are, you have to be willing to say, It's not in the best interests of my dogs to keep pushing. You pull back just to get through the race. And I finished twelfth.

It was a challenging race, but I didn't give up. So many dogs got sick. I had only nine dogs left. That was an important thing. I think I left Nikolai in almost fiftieth place. I had to regroup if I wanted to finish at all, or to have a shot at coming into Nome in the money. Finishing twelfth felt like a great accomplishment.

For the 2002 Iditarod I just tried to have a really low-key start, but I still don't think you can get behind and make up time. From the restart on, I ran my team at the speed I had trained them. They were running nice and steady, and I was passing teams and leaving them behind.

I passed Doug Swingley before Finger Lake. He was putting straw down for his dogs. I thought, Wow, that's kind of strange. No one's camped around here for a few years, and that's a different strategy for him. Oh well, that's not my strategy. And I kept on moving. Of course it was a different strategy for him because he didn't really race, just mushed on to Nome back in the pack.

I was a little surprised, but I wasn't going to worry about what he was doing. I've learned you can't worry about someone else's dog team or strategy. I just went along with my game plan.

Jon Little was parked near me, and I think Linwood Fiedler was out there. I was near the front but wasn't paying attention to anyone else. I did make one strategic error because I was going at such a fast pace. When I got to Rainy Pass, I had run less than 3½ hours and I had set the team to run 5½. But I stopped there and rested, and it threw me off my schedule. Martin Buser was on a different schedule. I never passed Martin when he was moving.

I should have kept going another two hours. I was pretty confident in my team even when Jon Little, John Baker, and DeeDee or Linwood went by. But when Martin went by I could see he was traveling similarly to how I was. Sometimes he was faster. And when he went by between Ophir and Cripple, I knew he had an advantage. When we left Cripple, he had two hours on me.

I thought I still had a shot at it. I caught Linwood and DeeDee about halfway to Cripple, and I thought, Wow, this is incredible. The way the dogs were moving, I thought I really could win, I just couldn't make any mistakes. I think it was pretty clear that Martin was the one to beat. There were still five hundred miles left in the race.

If you look at the history of the race, there have been teams within a couple of hours of the leader at the halfway point that started cutting rest, and they ended up twelve hours behind first. I was just going to continue running my race the way I planned it. I wanted to maintain my speed. I knew that the very second I began cutting rest, I would lose the advantage over the teams behind me.

I wasn't really losing ground on Martin, but I wasn't really gaining, either. I didn't look at it as if I was conceding first place right then. I was looking at it as though my only shot at winning was to maintain speed. If I blew up, I wouldn't even be second. I felt it was important to keep the dogs rested. I did go out of Elim within seven minutes of Martin, but I was still running my planned race. I had planned to go a little faster then, and take a short rest and then continue.

I guess the realization that I wasn't going to beat Martin unless something went wrong for him came to me when we were still on the Yukon River. I didn't lose hope. I was still trying. I just knew I couldn't make it up too easily. Maybe it was the conservative way to run the team, but that's how I like to run. I had already started thinking, What did I do wrong? What can I do better next year? How can I do this better next year, so it doesn't give an advantage to somebody else?

Some people said I was cutting rest at the end, but I rested just as long as I had planned. I went outside of Elim and got off the ice and then stopped, so it looked like I left chasing Martin, but my plan was to stop when we were off the ice. I rested thirty minutes, watering the dogs. I stuck with my plan and figured if it worked out, it worked out.

Martin set a new Iditarod record and broke nine days, and I finished second in 9 days, 49 minutes, 18 seconds. He beat me by two hours and ten minutes. Mine was the second fastest Iditarod ever, and it was exciting. I was kind of on an adrenaline high the second half of the race because I was so high up in the race. Everything was coming together.

I wasn't tired at the end of the race like I had been, and that comes down to the excitement at the end. I think if someone is coming hard it makes it exciting, and I think it's good for the race. If Martin got off the trail, or if he had any problems, two hours would be nothing. Then, all of a sudden, it would be a dead-even race. I knew fairly early on that he had a pretty good shot at holding me off, but there's always that chance when you're that close that something can happen.

I received a lot of congratulations, and family and friends were excited. People in the Native communities, where I get so much support, were saying that I could win it next. The Native support means a lot to me. I'm proud of where we come from. When I get to the Yukon River, it feels like I'm home. People there are always telling me to go catch those guys and win the race for them.

It's neat to have that support, and I feel a responsibility to give back. I've always felt that along with my mushing, I need to be a good citizen. There are a lot of issues facing the Native community today: alcoholism, teen suicide. I feel I have an obligation to show that no matter where you come from—whether there's alcoholism or domestic violence in your family, or you had a brother or sister who committed suicide, or you don't have as much money as the next guy—if you have a dream, you can achieve it.

My dream is to win the Iditarod. I haven't done it yet, but that's my dream. I can go out there and tell those kids I'm working hard, and it's through having a healthy lifestyle, staying away from drugs and alcohol, not smoking. Through hard work you can make dreams happen. To me, that's what running the Iditarod is all about.

My goal is to win the Iditarod—not just once, but several times. It's one step at a time. Whether I get rich at it as far as money goes, or not, I feel rich just being able to live the lifestyle we do. It's a struggle sometimes, but I think I appreciate where we're going and where we'll get to. If I do everything right and do what I know how to do, I think I have a good shot at beating any team out there.

RACE RECORD

1980	17 days, 7 hours, 59 minutes	24th
1981	16 days, 5 hours, 5 minutes	31st
1983	13 days, 18 hours, 10 minutes	15th
1984	15 days, 19 hours, 18 minutes	30th
1987	13 days, 2 hours, 58 minutes	22nd
1988	13 days, 16 hours, 29 minutes	9th
1989	11 days, 13 hours, 47 minutes	4th
1990	11 days, 14 hours, 41 minutes	5th
1991	13 days, 13 hours, 44 minutes	7th
1992	11 days, 9 hours, 5 minutes	5th
1993	10 days, 16 hours, 10 minutes	2nd
1994	11 days, 4 hours, 25 minutes	9th
1995	9 days, 11 hours, 24 minutes	4th
1996	9 days, 20 hours, 18 minutes	5th
1997	9 days, 18 hours, 26 minutes	4th
1998	9 days, 8 hours, 49 minutes	2nd
1999	Scratched	
2000	10 days, 4 hours, 24 minutes	20th
2001	11 days, 14 hours, 33 minutes	10th
2002	9 days, 22 hours, 7 minutes	16th
2003	10 days, 23 hours, 45 minutes	18th

CHAPTER 24
DEEDEE JONROWE

After more than two decades of long-distance racing, DeeDee Jonrowe, fifty, of Willow, Alaska, is one of the most popular mushers in the Iditarod Trail Sled Dog Race. Jonrowe has been a race institution since 1980.

Jonrowe began competitive mushing when she and her husband, Mike, lived in Bethel, Alaska, but she was first exposed to the sport as a student at the University of Alaska Fairbanks.

Her best Iditarod finish is second, twice, but perhaps her most dramatic high finish occurred in 1997. Jonrowe placed fourth, only months after an automobile accident severely injured her and her husband and killed her grandmother. The indispensable training help of former world champion sprint musher Roxy Wright enabled Jonrowe to compete, and solidified a sister-like bond between the mushers.

Jonrowe has developed a deep fan base. She is renowned for her toughness and graciousness and is deeply religious. After the car accident, thousands of Alaskans wrote messages of cheer to DeeDee and Mike Jonrowe, and did so once again in 2002 when Jonrowe was diagnosed with breast cancer. At the time Jonrowe spoke about her Iditarod career, she was undergoing chemotherapy treatment.

Just about my first time mushing a dog team came about because Iditarod racer John Cooper was dating a girlfriend of mine when I lived in Fairbanks. When he wasn't home, I hooked up his five trapline dogs to one of those little plastic flyer sleds and took off. It didn't take them long to pitch me off. The team was lost for two days, and I didn't know how I was going to tell Coop that I'd lost his dog team.

John came back before the dogs did, and he was kind of known for his temper. This was one of my best girlfriends, and I thought she should tell him. She wasn't up for that at all. We finally got them back—they got tangled up in a fence, but nobody was really hurt, thank goodness. I made every mistake you could make, including hooking up somebody else's dog team when he wasn't there.

I never could have imagined that I would be mushing the Iditarod for more than twenty years. But there was an innate attraction to the lifestyle. In recent years, the Iditarod has created its own world. There weren't many people who could do it full-time. It was more of a supplementary event that was done as an annex to the rest of your life.

The guys who were commercial fishermen might mush in the winter, or guys I knew hunted, fished, and picked berries for subsistence and ran dogs in the winter. The idea of a full-time emphasis on the Iditarod wasn't part of the environment I knew in Bethel. The first Iditarod musher I knew was Myron Angstman, and he was a lawyer. That was his full-time profession, and he was a good dog driver.

I had the chance to do the Kuskokwim 300 back in Bethel in 2002, and I loved it. I just love the people. It was a homecoming. It was the closest thing to a home reunion I've ever had in my life. People were stopping us on the street, and Mike and I were being invited to lunch. We headed over to our old house, which we realized we hadn't lived in for fifteen years. It's where we met. We have some really special friends there.

I finished third in the Kusko, and it was funny at one point because Charlie Boulding and I were lying down on a break and some of the others started racing again, and he said, "We have to

let the young pups go. That's oldness."

Charlie and I had a lot of fun racing, and it turns out we're racing another race right now, together. We're both dealing with cancer. When you're trying to continue on with your lifestyle and trying to make sure you don't get an infection, and also squeezing in a kazillion doctor's visits, it's hard.

At first I just wanted to finish the Iditarod. My attitude changed when I got my first top-ten finish in 1988. Mike was working full-time, and I had only twenty-five dogs. By then Susan Butcher and I had become friends, and she was helping me know more about how to accomplish things. I don't think Susan ever had any intention of teaching me how to beat her. But she was interested in helping me to be better, and to be able to race closer to her where we could be friends on the trail, too. I'll always thank her for that, because it takes a special personality to allow a potential competitor in.

The top ten was a milestone. I went from knowing I could reach the top ten to having the goal of making the top five. That year, I was stuck in a storm in a cabin at the fish camp between Shaktoolik and Koyuk with Jerry Austin, Rick Mackey, and Lavon Barve for a couple of days. We were constantly watching the weather to try to get out of there and keep our little jump on the mushers behind us. I was so thankful for making the top ten for the first time. I felt like I was in very special company for the first time.

Then I had my first second-place finish in 1993. I really thought I was going to be third. Mackey and Jeff King and I were choo-chooing from Golovin to White Mountain. But then Rick said,

"My team is faltering. I'm not going to be able to chase you guys out of here. So it's you and Jeff."

I began thinking, What can I make happen here? Jeff and I were only six minutes apart when we left White Mountain. We were catching Jeff's team some in the hills, but when he hit the flats he had overdrive.

When I came down off the Topkok Hills, I could see him and I asked the dogs for more. They gave me that look of, "You've got to be kidding. We've already given you everything." I realized I was not going to get first place. We were forty miles from the finish, and I was not in position to ask my dogs for more. They were giving me the max.

I finished thirty-two minutes behind, but it was a very satisfying finish. It was probably one of the neatest nights of my racing career. My grandmother from Virginia was there, and she has since died. Both of my grandmothers have. I did more than anybody had ever expected from me, even I from myself, and I was so thrilled with that placing.

My second time finishing in second place, in 1998, I wasn't as happy because I wanted more.

After coming so close in 1993, I felt I was close to being able to win, but it didn't happen. It took five years to even get second again. I have learned to kind of place caution on my expectations and do the very best I can. I never think that I know all the answers. I'm still always looking for the cutting-edge thing to do.

I had a fantastic team in 1998. The dogs peaked just right. They were feeling good. I had leaders who were really responsive. I ran Commander in single lead an awful lot. He did the whole Yukon River in single lead and led the whole race there. I think that was pretty hard on him mentally.

The biggest move that I made that year was not taking my twenty-four-hour layover until I reached Ophir. That gave me a little bit of a jump on everybody—everybody except John Baker. They didn't count on my making as long a run as I made. I broke my run into two, from Ophir to Cripple and Cripple to Ruby, and then camped. When Martin Buser went by, it was the first team I'd seen all night. He said, "Good move, girl," and soon he had to stop. He had to take a break, and I was ready to come off an eight-hour rest. So I got to Ruby four hours ahead of everyone else. I maintained that lead until Jeff King did the same kind of thing. He skipped Galena and split his run into Nulato.

Kaltag was the last checkpoint I pulled into first. I thought I had taken command of the race in Kaltag until I realized what Jeff had done, and then I knew it was a fight. It was a war, and we really knocked heads leaving Koyuk.

Jeff came over and said he needed six hours there and that nobody else could follow us out with that rest. It had been really storming on the Bering Sea coast, and I didn't want to topple my team. I didn't want to sit there and let everyone else pile up on me. I figured I could at least get second, if I just let Jeff go. I thought that if he had to break trail the whole way, maybe his leaders would fold on him. But he hasn't misjudged those dogs often. I didn't want to go on that gamble. Maybe it was wrong, maybe it was right. I knew that I had enough trouble getting my leaders, Commander and Job, to take care of their own business, never mind playing head games with Jeff.

The first time I finished second, I never led. This race I had led quite a bit, so I wasn't as happy. But it was the best race I could run that year. In twenty-some Iditarods, you're going to have good years and bad years. In 2002 I had a fabulous dog team, but I finished sixteenth. I honestly believe, from what the doctors' reports said, that I was actively dealing with cancer and didn't know it. I was fighting endurance problems that come from that, and it kicked me. I was wearing down during the race, and I was hospitalized for thirty-six hours when I got to Nome.

I was just completely dehydrated. We didn't know what was wrong, but I took six bags of fluid. I've always been tired at the finish, but this was much more than that. It had never been to the point where I was hospitalized. I always bounce back quickly. That was certainly not the case, and I think this cancer had to do with it. I definitely believe I'd been fighting it. The race ended in March, and I received the cancer diagnosis in July.

The two second-place finishes were special, but my fourth place in 1997 after the car accident is probably my favorite race. That was an achievement. I believe I was counted out, and right-fully so. Mike couldn't stand on his own for four months, and my grandmother died. I was injured. We had insurance problems and money problems because of it. To me, that is testimony that if you turn things over to God, God can deal with them. You've got to turn them over. He's always there working with you.

I wasn't sure what I could do. All I knew was that the race was a kind of healing, that I felt best when I was with the dogs. It was my spiritual time. That was my time to talk to God, and it was my time to receive positive feedback from my dogs.

To me, the dogs were an example of God's unconditional love: in spite of all the things that had happened, they were there for me. They seemed to have an innate knowledge that they needed to be a little gentler and not whack me around much. When I left Takotna, I had the smallest dog team in the race. Susan Butcher was there, and I said, "Well, you know, I've been training small dog teams all winter because that's all my strength can handle." And I took my ten-dog team all the way to Nome. I don't think anyone expected me to finish fourth. Some people said, "You shouldn't even race."

I'm hearing the same feedback now: "Your chemotherapy won't even be done until a month before the race. Take a break. Nobody will think differently about you if you don't make it this year."

The accident occurred in October 1996. We were driving on the Parks Highway, on the way home from the dog mushers' symposium in Fairbanks. I suffered a ruptured small intestine and an injured left shoulder in a head-on collision. I was stuck in the car for ninety minutes before they got me out, and it took longer to rescue Mike. My grandmother, Mildred Stout, was dying next to me. Mike was unconscious, and I was afraid he was going to die.

At the hospital in Fairbanks, the switchboard was jammed. The flowers were just amazing; we shared them with patients throughout the hospital. The state of Alaska really rallied to our sides. That was particularly nice because we have a small family. Mike's dad sat with him, and my mom sat with me. Friends rallied around and made up the extended family it took to get well. Prayer chains were started everywhere. A lot of people showed that they cared. We were very humbled by it. My major sponsors were very supportive at the time, too.

That winter I could not physically train a dog team the way I normally would. Roxy Wright stepped up and went 100 percent to develop a dog team for me. She took my dogs to her home in Fairbanks. Her specialty is short races, but her expertise is dogs. Roxy knows her stuff.

The accident happened on October 27, and I was told that I could not step on the runners of a dogsled until December 6. They said that was the magic date of healing. On that day, I arrived in Fairbanks and went over to Susan Butcher's house. Susan and Roxy had all of the dogs ready for me, and I ran a team. A couple of days later, we loaded my dogs in the truck and drove them home to Willow. Roxy stayed with me for two weeks.

I was wondering what I was doing out there. My life was in such disarray. I believe I was out there because God was teaching me. He was rebuilding my strength. He was rebuilding me into the position that He had for me. I think that's one of the reasons I've never questioned whether or not I am called to this sport.

You always want your life to mean something, and I want to know that when I leave this earth my life meant something, that it wasn't just about personal, selfish pursuit. I believe that my life has meant something in this sport. I may never win the Iditarod, but I'm certainly pursuing it, and once again, with this cancer, I am having one of those years where I have to dig super deep to get there.

Maybe this philosophy means something to people in Alaska. They certainly aren't responding to someone who is a constant champion. I've had a lot of successful races. I've had some high-profile unsuccessful races. But people still seem to respond to me.

I believe people respond to me because I really care. I care that my life makes a difference. I care that if there is something I can do that will help a situation, I will try to do that. I care that our young people in the villages don't get lost in the fraying of cultures; they are really important to me. I see them potentially lost in a world of mixed cultures that leaves them with no goals. They need to have pride in their culture, as well as being able to make a go of it in a cash economy. They need both.

In the 1997 race, I was taking it a checkpoint at a time. I didn't know how strong I was. I didn't know how competitive I could be. When I got back up near the front group, everybody was very, very nice to me. The others weren't expecting to see me that year, but they were glad to see me.

When I finished in fourth place, I felt as if I had won. I had won, in a personal way. I had spent a lot of time on the trail with my grandmother. I had not had any grieving time for her because I couldn't go to the funeral. I didn't have the time reflecting on her life and what a positive person she was.

I could see her singing in the chorus in heaven—she always sang in the choir. It was a very special moment for me. It was a release. Early on in the race, I thought about scratching because it was just too much. I just didn't feel like I wanted to be away from Mike for two weeks. I had almost lost him, and I didn't want to be apart. If I had done that, it would have taken me another whole year to purge. But I kept saying to myself, "I'll just go to the next checkpoint and make my decision there."

People were amazed when I finished fourth, but they should only be amazed in the power of God. I did surprise myself. That was one of my greatest racing achievements. The odds weren't good. A lot of people don't think the odds are too good that I will be able to race the 2003 Iditarod.

I have been hearing from a lot of people who fought the battle and came out the other side, and I have heard from relatives of people who fought the battle and lost. They all say that it's critical to them that I fight the battle and win. And that's my intention. I would love to win the Iditarod this time. I don't know if it's at all possible, because of my own personal strength. To have surgery, that's one thing, but to have six months of chemotherapy and have it constantly knock you down, that's another thing. I'll deal with it and I'll fight it as best I can. I have every intention of being at the starting line.

I think the race scene will invigorate me. It never crossed my mind not to enter the Iditarod. It crossed everybody else's mind, once again, but the only reason I would not go is if I didn't feel I could hang onto the team and would therefore be putting my dogs at risk by losing the team in places.

You develop a different strategy. You come at it from a different direction. The dogs I take may not be the best-trained dogs, but they will be the most responsive. They may not necessarily be the fastest, but they will cling to me more. It will keep me out of trouble.

Sometimes I get mad because I got breast cancer. I've been pretty unhappy about it. I was not at all prepared to think this was something I would have to deal with. We've never seen it in our family. And the more I read about it, the less I understand how I got it—how, and why. There are times when I have told Mike, "I don't want to do this. I don't want to do this cancer treatment."

I don't have kids, and if I didn't have Mike, maybe I wouldn't do it. I would just take my odds and go on because I feel like I've been sick so long. But he doesn't deserve that. He's all I've got, and I'm all he's got. Some days I feel sorry for myself and I don't feel like doing it. But I do it.

It knocks me out. It's just a depressing feeling, but when a day goes by and I've gotten through it, then I think, OK, well, all right. There are a lot of people in cancer treatment with me, and I think, Well, those guys are doing it. I certainly have things I would like to do.

The Iditarod is a family, and in most cases those of us who have been doing it for a long time have seen our competitors marry and raise their families, and, in some cases, seen their family in competition with us. We've seen divorces. We've seen parents die. We've lived through a lot of things. We've lived through a lot of successes with one another, and a lot of personal tragedies.

We've now seen Joe Redington Sr. come and go, and there's a whole era of us still going who raced with him and knew him in the early days, and we're still here. We'll see Col. Norman Vaughan go in that direction some day—he's 98—but he just shocked me the other day when he said, "We have unfinished business." We have a deal that I will win the Iditarod before he turns one hundred. I said, "We're making this harder and harder on ourselves, Norman."

It really is quite a feeling of family, even when you run your heart out to compete against someone. It's evolved to the point where it's just a season's race, but your competitors are still family, with their losses, ups and downs, and personality traits that you either like or don't like. They're still family, and you still love them.

Martin Buser's family has been cooking meals for us. Charlie and Robin Boulding wrote to me right away when they heard about the cancer. They're going through the same thing with Charlie's colon cancer, and they wouldn't wish it on anyone. So we're uplifting each other.

Lance Mackey had cancer, and in 2002 he started the Iditarod. He called and said, "I don't feel sorry for you. I feel BAD. I don't want you to have to do this." All I kept thinking about was what a hero Lance was. The fact that he didn't finish the Iditarod but did make a racing season out of it was incredible to me. Just absolutely incredible. Bill Cotter has been there for me. And Vern Halter. He's been encouraging me. I think the world of Vern.

I heard from John Baker. He makes me laugh. He's got the best sense of humor. Joe Garnie called. And Mike Williams. My friends from the villages are pretty valuable to me. I'm hearing from a lot of people, and it's inspirational.

They are your aunts and uncles and siblings. They're your friends. They'll be your staunch competitors come March, but they're also your friends.

[DeeDee Jonrowe entered the 2003 Iditarod and, running a steady pace, finished eighteenth—her sixteenth time earning top-twenty money.]

ABOUT THE AUTHOR

Lew Freedman is the author of many books about Alaska, including *Iditarod Classics; Father of the Iditarod: The Joe Redington Story; Iditarod Dreams* with DeeDee Jonrowe; *One Second to Glory* with Dick Mackey; and *Spirit of the Wind: The George Attla Story.*

CPSIA information can be obtained at www.ICGtesting.com
264802BV00006B/4/P

9 780972 494489